P9-EMC-807

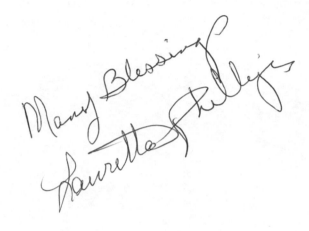

Many Blessings

Lauretta Phillips

A Closer Walk

ONE WOMAN'S JOURNEY

—— *Lauretta Phillips* ——

WESTBOW
PRESS®
A DIVISION OF THOMAS NELSON
& ZONDERVAN

Copyright © 2016 Lauretta Phillips.

All rights reserved. No part of this book may be used or reproduced by any means, graphic, electronic, or mechanical, including photocopying, recording, taping or by any information storage retrieval system without the written permission of the author except in the case of brief quotations embodied in critical articles and reviews.

This book is a work of non-fiction. Unless otherwise noted, the author and the publisher make no explicit guarantees as to the accuracy of the information contained in this book and in some cases, names of people and places have been altered to protect their privacy.

All Scripture quotations in this publications are from The Message. Copyright © by Eugene H. Peterson 1993, 1994, 1995, 1996, 2000, 2001, 2002. Used by permission of NavPress Publishing Group.

Scripture taken from the Holy Bible, NEW INTERNATIONAL VERSION®. Copyright © 1973, 1978, 1984 by Biblica, Inc. All rights reserved worldwide. Used by permission. NEW INTERNATIONAL VERSION® and NIV® are registered trademarks of Biblica, Inc. Use of either trademark for the offering of goods or services requires the prior written consent of Biblica US, Inc.

Scripture quotations taken from the New American Standard Bible®, Copyright © 1960, 1962, 1963, 1968, 1971, 1972, 1973, 1975, 1977, 1995 by The Lockman Foundation. Used by permission. (www.Lockman.org)

Scripture taken from the *Amplified Bible*, copyright © 1954, 1958, 1962, 1964, 1965, 1987 by The Lockman Foundation. Used by permission.

WestBow Press books may be ordered through booksellers or by contacting:

WestBow Press
A Division of Thomas Nelson & Zondervan
1663 Liberty Drive
Bloomington, IN 47403
www.westbowpress.com
1 (866) 928-1240

Because of the dynamic nature of the Internet, any web addresses or links contained in this book may have changed since publication and may no longer be valid. The views expressed in this work are solely those of the author and do not necessarily reflect the views of the publisher, and the publisher hereby disclaims any responsibility for them.

Any people depicted in stock imagery provided by Thinkstock are models, and such images are being used for illustrative purposes only.
Certain stock imagery © Thinkstock.

ISBN: 978-1-5127-2980-1 (sc)
ISBN: 978-1-5127-2981-8 (hc)
ISBN: 978-1-5127-2979-5 (e)

Library of Congress Control Number: 2016901888

Print information available on the last page.

WestBow Press rev. date: 02/11/2016

Contents

Dedication

Dedication: This book is dedicated to Sherry Isabella who went to be with the Lord before this book was completed. It is because of her dedication and love for God and her intense need to know and because of the questions of others like her that this book is written.

Acknowledgements

Special thanks go to Anne-Marie Forer whose editing and suggestions were superb and without whom, I might never have completed this book.

To Larry whose encouragement and support helped to make this possible, and to my daughter Lesa whose love and support kept me moving forward. Thanks to my sisters Carol and Cora and family and friends who believed in me and kept encouraging me to get this done.

Preface

I was sitting in church one day and a woman I had not met before sat down beside me. I had been coming to this church off and on for about a year. She was new. We got into a conversation about how welcome the people made you feel. We talked about being new to church and about her being a new Christian. After the service, she asked me if I did a Bible Study. I said I studied every day on my own but would love to study with others as well. She said she would like that. Could we get together?

The pastor had indicated that he would like to see some small group studies taking place, so I suggested that we talk to him about it. We waited until he had finished shaking hands with the line of people and I introduced him to Sherry and told him of her request. He said he would put together a Bible study. We decided to begin meeting the following Tuesday and to invite others to join us. From that chance meeting at church a friendship blossomed.

Sherry was hungry for the Word. She wanted an in-depth personal study. Twice more she asked me about studying His Word with me. Each time something got in the way of doing a one-on-one study. It seemed apparent that God was not giving me a Bible study to lead. So what was He giving me?

Many others over the course of the year asked me about studying God's Word. They said the same thing that Sherry did, "I just want to get to know God better. I just want a closer walk with God."

I don't know why they asked me about it, but every time someone did it was a draw on my heart. I wanted to find a way to help. I have a heart for God and want to do His will. If it wasn't His will for me to lead a Bible study, then what was His will?

Finally, I was having my quiet time with God and writing in my journal like I do almost every morning and God said, "I have given you this writing ability for a purpose." I said, "I know God. I have no natural ability to speak or write. Without you I could not do this." He said, "Write the book."

What? Which book? Over the years I have written essays, magazine stories and articles, short stories for anthologies, newspaper articles, and many stories to tell. The writing is God's gift. He has given me a sense of humor and a writing style that I could not have developed on my own.

During this time my storytelling work slowed down and God was giving me time to write. I knew He was anointing me to write something. I just kept asking, "What? Which book?"

Finally, I decided to pray for God's divine guidance. I prayed for Him to give me a discerning spirit and the wisdom to see and know the truth. His words came loud and clear, "Just a Closer Walk." I wrote it in my journal. It was confirmed the next Sunday when another woman asked me about learning to walk closer to God. God didn't tell me to hold a Bible study or to lead a group, He told me to write this book.

Without Sherry and her first question and without the others that confirmed the question, this journey would not have begun. Without God's direction this book would not be written.

For years I studied God's word and listened for that still small voice. Eventually I came to know the secret of God's love, the secret that God wants me to share with you.

As you read this book, I pray that you too will ask for discernment and wisdom to know the truth. I pray that you will find your own path and one day will say as I do, "Every day in every way I walk hand in hand with God." On those days when I am not walking, I know I can climb onto the lap of the Father and lean on Him. I know I am loved and accepted into the family of God, adopted as His child.

I say as Paul says in Ephesians 1:15-18

> Every time I prayed; I'd think of you and give thanks. But I do more than give thanks, I ask – ask that you can see exactly what it is He is calling you to do, grasp the immensity of this glorious way of life He has for His followers. Oh, the utter extravagance of His work in us who trust Him – endless energy, boundless strength. (MES)

CHAPTER 1

Just a Closer Walk

The Journey

Just a closer walk with thee.
Grant it Jesus is my plea.
Daily walking close to thee.
Let it be dear Lord. Let it be.

This has been a favorite song of mine for a long time. I couldn't find any reference to the original author of this song. The earliest reference was way back prior to the Civil War. Songs with similar lyrics were published in the early 1800s. In the 1940s the popular version of this song was arranged and published by Kenneth Morris. He added some new lyrics and a choral arrangement. Since the 1940s many versions of this song have emerged. It is included in most of the hymnals of today.

When God gave me this title I began thinking about this song. I realized this was a very personal song for me. I have been singing it since I was a small child. It was a prayer uttered in desperation. It was a song of hope and joy. I often find myself singing this song even when I do not know why.

Getting to know God has been a very personal journey for me. Sometimes it is difficult to share the faltering steps. Other times I can't help but smile at God's great sense of humor and the laughter and joy He has allowed me to share with others.

My journey actually began when I was ten years old. I accepted Christ as my personal savior in July 1953 at Rock Lake Christian Camp. I was baptized that same evening during the vesper services at the lake. My parents thought I was too young to make such a decision, but from that point on, I knew God was with me.

It was a good thing He was because life as I knew it changed radically. Life has a way of happening, and things change when you are least expecting them to--and for me, life happened.

God was always there--sometimes in the background and sometimes as a major feature in my life. The years between 1953 and 1987 flew by. I often found myself in crisis mode. Some of my experiences are too terrifying to tell and the telling of those stories would not serve the purpose of this book.

I became independent and I was sure I could find a way to take care of myself. I found myself on my knees often during those desperate times. I lived basically in crisis mode from the time I was eleven until I was thirty, moving from one difficult situation to another. After having some health issues caused by stress, I decided I needed to change things up a bit and life got better. I didn't take things so seriously, and I learned to have fun along the way. I learned to laugh again and to enjoy life more.

I have been keeping journals since I was about nine years old. I don't have them all. Some were burned in a fire, and the earlier ones just got lost somehow along the way. Looking back at these journal entries helps me see just how far I have really come.

I usually start a new journal on the first day of each New Year and write in it until space runs out. I often have more than one journal for each year. I don't do New Year's resolutions, but I do set some goals and make a to-do list. Getting to know God better topped my list for 1987. It was on the top of my list again in January 1988. It wasn't until 1989 that I was actually conscious of intentionally taking the steps that would lead me closer to Him.

Here are some of the steps I took along this journey and excerpts from my journals written during those years. I have decided to share some of these journal entries with you. Hopefully it will help you to understand your own journey better.

⬯⬯⬯

Journal Entry

January 1989

I climbed the stairs to my apartment over the garage and put my bag on the chair by the table. The apartment is small but big enough for me. Two bedrooms, a bathroom, a kitchen, a dining/living room, a garage to put my car in and a laundry/craft room downstairs.

It was quite late when I stopped at the bar for dinner and conversation with my friends and now it's even later. The "friends" were into their own thing. I really don't do drama and drunks well so I sat up at the bar and talked with one of the owners who over the years has become a good friend.

I started going to this bar/restaurant for meals when I bought the building next door and I felt welcome and at home here. The food is good. The people are friendly and I soon was playing on the shuffle board team and meeting a few friends after work. But now I don't live next door. The divorce that I didn't want has forced the sale of the building and I have moved from pillar to post and now I live out in the country in a rented apartment.

Shuffle board season is over and I have pretty much quit drinking so just hanging out at the bar isn't what I want to do. I decided not to drink so much when I found myself wanting a drink as a way to relax when I got out of work each night.

One Saturday I woke up after having a late Friday night out with the girls and thought "This must be the way alcoholics get started. I am not going to be an alcoholic like my dad." My dad died of complications from alcoholism in 1972. I quit drinking. It wasn't as easy as I thought it was going to be. My friends often bought me a drink and had it waiting for me when I got there after work. I had to make arrangements with the owners and bartender not to let them do that. I didn't want to give up my friends, I just wanted to quit drinking so much. When they insisted I have a drink with them, I had to ask them to make it a tonic and lime. Eventually they understood but they didn't think I drank too much. "After all I didn't drink as much as they did and they weren't alcoholics were they?" It was like trying to lose weight and having everyone bring you dessert. Now I have an occasional drink but mostly drink tonic water and lime.

Work as a retail manager is very stressful, especially in the fashion industry. Management means 70 or 80 hours a week and it also means always being on someone's "list". I am good at it but it is starting to get me down. I wish I were back at the bookstore or at my own store.

My life is pretty mundane for an active woman and tomorrow will be another long day just like this one. Work 12 hours, stop for dinner and come home to nothing.

I do have other things I love to do like making stained glass things, quilting, and writing and now I have added storytelling to the list. Those things have to wait until one of those rare days come along when I find time to do them. I put the leftovers from dinner in the refrigerator and decided to climb into bed. I find myself once again crying out my loneliness and pain to God and writing it in this journal. Writing helps and talking to God about it helps more.

⚬⚬⚬

So began this journey. It has not been an easy one but I would not trade it. The joy and fulfillment my life has held is more than I ever imagined.

I am still walking out this journey. I am getting closer to Him all the time. I am not finished with this walk. I am sure I will never be finished learning more about Him until the day I meet Him face to face. I do know I am growing from glory to glory.

It is my hope that somehow this path I have been on will touch your life with insight and wisdom as you continue on your own journey. I hope that you will reach out your hand to His and call Him Father. I hope that one day you too will climb upon His lap, rest there, and lean on Him.

I suggest you keep a journal of your own journey, one you can look back on and say "Oh yes! That is when I learned that." Bring God into your everyday life. Ask questions, and find the places you will learn from. Take notes and look up the references and quotes.

Growing is painful and often times funny but I always think in the end it is worth every step. I hope you think so too. Enjoy the journey.

CHAPTER 2

Who's On First?

I knew that as soon as I made the decision to get to know God and have a closer walk with Him, the enemy would do everything in his power to distract or defeat me.

It is sometimes an outright attack but often it is subtle. For instance, I would decide to go to church. Suddenly, someone would call in sick and I would have to go to work instead.

I decided that part of my journey was to set aside a portion of each day in my life for quiet time with God. That is harder to do than you might think. That's when the phone rings. It is often someone you feel you really need to talk with. Then someone comes to the door, and you know they know you are home. Hiding in the bathroom won't do it. You have to answer. It turns out to be your lonely neighbor. She is the one who talks really fast so she can say everything she has on her mind. Only she never gets quite done. She sees that the coffee pot is on, so she goes to the cupboard and gets a cup. She says she can only stay a minute. About a half hour later, you interrupt to say you are busy. She excuses herself, and fifteen minutes later she leaves. You know she is lonely and needs to talk. You feel a bit guilty about cutting her visit short, but you still want your quiet time with God.

You are heading towards your meditation corner when you pass by a mirror and discover your hair is really a mess. You stop to comb it, and you realize you still haven't gotten dressed. Then you think you really need a shower before you get dressed, so you take a shower. Now that you are all clean, you can get back to what you were going to do. What was that? Oh yeah, meditation. Time is almost gone.

One of the great lies that the enemy uses to distract us is that we are all really busy. Being busy makes us feel important. The enemy says you are too busy to spend time with God right now, wait until later. Maybe you will have time after work or just before bed.

<hr>

Journal entry

March 1989,

I woke to the sound of the telephone this morning. The mall security called to tell me to stay home. The mall was closed and I would not be able to open the store today. I got up and got my schedule. Called my Regional Director to let her know and then called the scheduled employees and told them to not come in. It's tough because I know they all need the hours. Shorter paychecks just are not in anyone's budget and as much as I would like to change it, retail just doesn't pay very well. I did all that before the coffee got done! Now what? I had tons of work to do. The store displays needed to be redone before the weekend. We needed to get ready for inventory. The back room needs to be re-organized. The list goes on and on. Being a manager and assistant to the district manager means there is a lot to do and I find myself going over the list. I am way too busy to take a snow day.

But wait!! What an unexpected reprieve! Just last night I was wishing I had more time. I got myself another cup of coffee.

I love sitting in this arm chair by the window having my morning coffee. I love the quiet time between dark and dawn when the night sounds have stopped and the dawn chorus has not started. The sun is just rising and I can watch the glow on the horizon and suddenly above all this white, there is a red ball popping up like a balloon. The effect on the snow is stunning. God sure has made a beautiful world for us to enjoy. Just think, I could have been at work and missed it all!

The female cardinal comes to the window and lands on the ledge. I think she is surprised that I am home. I have never had a bird pay so much attention to me before. She flies to whatever window I am at. If I am here she comes by to say hello. If I am in the kitchen cooking or washing up she taps on the window to let me know she is there. I have never heard of a bird doing that before. All God's creatures…

There it is again. God showing up. I have been straying away from Him quite a bit for the past 3 or 4 years. On the top of my "To Do List" for 1988 was to have a closer walk with God and get to know Him better. It was on my "to do" list for this year too! I guess He is taking me up on that request this year. He seems to be popping up everywhere I look. Or maybe I am just noticing Him more.

Today would be a good day to reflect and re-evaluate what I am doing and how I am living. I certainly am not happy with things the way they are. I am alone once again. This time against my will. Another failed marriage. Another failed relationship. But I am not going to sit here today and have a pity party. I have had enough of those lately. I was listening to Joyce Meyers on the radio the other day and she said "You can be pitiful or powerful but you can't be pitiful and powerful." I guess I choose to be powerful from now on. Time to get back to that walk with God I have been wishing for.

It seems I have always had God in my life. Sometimes I put Him on a shelf and leave Him there until I am in trouble and really need Him to rescue me. Sometimes I bring Him out and let Him have a major role in my life. Like when I was raising Lesa and we were involved in church and Sunday school and youth group. Then I turned my back and walked away as though it was my choice when God showed up.

My idea of what God is and can do needs some revision I think. I find I am reading my Bible more often. Perhaps that is why I am noticing Him more? I find myself praying more too! Different than those "Help me" prayers too. Not that it is the only way I prayed in the past. I prayed for people and situations and things like that. I prayed when others needed help and for peace in the world and for the country as a whole. Now my prayers seem to be more personal. As though I am really talking to Him!

Father God, I love you. Father God, I need you. Father… That's it!

Father. He is the Father I have been hunting for. The one who is always there for me whenever I need Him. The one who wants a predominate place in my life. The one who deserves my respect and love more than anything else in my life. The one who loves me so much He gave His only Son!

<hr />

In the beginning, I did not realize that having good things happen could also be a way to distract me from doing what I needed to get to know God better.

The promotion at work is a nice surprise, but it means more time on the job and less time with family, friends and God. The raise in pay is great, but is it worth it? You get invited to join a board of a non-profit or a group. It is an honor. It only meets once a month. You can spare that time, can't you?

Today, as it happens on many days when I am writing, I find myself distracted. The phone rings. It is my daughter who should be at work so I answer knowing something is not right. She is home from work having trouble with her rheumatoid arthritis and she wants to talk. I love talking with her and I don't think I do that often enough, but I excuse myself after a half hour and begin writing again. The phone rings again. This time it is a storyteller who needs to discuss a job we are doing together. Soon it is noon and I have not had breakfast yet. I know I need to go to the bank and the grocery store this afternoon.

But wait! I have committed to working on this book at least two hours every day. If I don't, I feel as though I have let myself and God down. I need to make a decision to keep my commitments.

God gave me directions for this book. He is the inspiration for it. I need to stick to my commitment. The bank and groceries can wait. We won't starve, and the bank will not go broke without our deposit. I need to put God first. So, I shut off the phone, pull the drapes so no one can tell if I am here, and settle back down to work.

Suddenly I am smiling and I am inspired. It is that way with this. Putting God first is one of the lessons I am learning over and over again. Making a conscious decision to intentionally obey God makes my heart sing.

Listen, I am not saying you will never have troubles, or be tempted to do something that is not walking the way of our Lord. I am not even saying you will recognize some of the subtle temptations, or even think of resisting them. What I am saying is that to have a closer walk with God we need to spend time with Him.

You cannot maintain a relationship with someone you never talk with. Relationships take work. We are the children of God. You cannot maintain a relationship with a Father you never talk with.

Galatians 4:4-7

> But when the fullness of the time came, God sent forth His Son, born of a woman, born under the Law, so that He might redeem those who were under the Law, that we might receive the adoption as sons. Because you are sons, God has sent forth the Spirit of His Son into our hearts crying "ABBA! FATHER! Therefore you are no longer a slave but a son and if a son then an heir through God. (NAS)

As you begin your walk with God your Father, pay attention to what is going on around you. What is happening to interrupt or delay your alone time with God?

Use a journal to mark your time with the Father. Journal about your emotions and your day. Read your journal periodically to see where and when those things happen that put you over the edge. When is it that you are too busy? What and who are your interruptions?

What can you do to change those things that are blocking or interrupting your journey? Is there some way you can change your schedule, or do something different to make sure you have some quiet time with God? Do you have a place you can be by yourself with God? Make yourself a quiet space you can go to whenever you want or need alone time with God. Make it comfortable, peaceful and quiet. Sometimes soft music helps.

I have a couple spaces. One is an old rocker in a corner by the fire place where I can watch the sun come up and the day begin. I go there early when my guy is off to work or out in the barn. I sometimes find myself there in the middle of the day just watching the mountains and talking with God.

Another space is my office. I use it for work. It houses my desk and files, computers and recording equipment, a small sofa bed (for guests) lots of books and my sewing things. I have to be determined when I go there if I am going to spend time with God. It is pretty easy to get caught up in the minutiae of day-to-day activities on the computer, and with my other work instead. It does serve the purpose though and can be the right space when I shut the door and keep out any interruptions.

If I am traveling I often use my car. I sit in a parking lot or driveway and listen to the still small voice that gives me courage to keep going for another day.

Start your day with God and end your day with God. He is the First and the Last, the Alpha and the Omega, the Beginning and the End. He is the Father we have been yearning for. He yearns to spend time with you.

CHAPTER 3

Who Am I Anyway?

I have lived in dozens of places and at least twenty-eight states. I have had five different careers and done many outrageous things. But do those places I have lived and the different things I have done define who I am?

They helped me to become who I am for sure, but do they define who I am on the inside? Can people look at me and say she did this or that? Or she is this or that? Can they tell that I once rode motor cycles and flew airplanes? Do they know that I have had cancer five times or that I wanted twelve kids and had one? Can they tell I am a writer or a storyteller? Can they tell that I am a child of the King?

∞

Journal Entry

June 1990

Wow another adventure. Drove to New Hampshire to come to my sister Cora Jo and John Ciampi's wedding and bring her son Charley back home to stay with me for a couple of weeks while they honeymoon and get used to each other. She was a mail order bride or at least that is what I am calling her. She met

John through an ad in the *Backwoods Home* magazine. It was all my "old" sister's fault. She said "I will write to some of these guys if you do." Cora did! Funny thing though, that magazine was a year old.

John and Cora have been writing and calling and visiting each other for over a year and she decided to give up her career and home in Montana to come here to marry him. Big decision for her. Lots of prayers went into that.

What a beautiful place this State is. I love the mountains.

My nephew is excited to show me around these hills and woods near John's place. The area here was started as a hippie community back in the sixties. Each person purchased their own land and built their own house. The idea was to all help each other as a community. One by one the people sold their places until there were only three of the original families left. John didn't build his house but he did buy it rather early on so they were essentially a part of the community from almost the beginning.

We were wandering around in the woods yesterday when we came into this clearing. Charley said "You are going to love this place Aunt Gert" and sure enough he was right.

I headed right for the rock wall that surrounded the "used to be" garden. In the center was a large rock and I went over and set down in the sunshine. I love sitting on rocks. There was some asparagus going to seed against one part of the garden wall. Outside the garden and in the center of the clearing was an octagon shaped shack. It looked as though it had seen its better days yet there was something compelling about it. The doors were ajar and it looked abandoned. Charley wasn't sure who owned it but he knew they were from out of State and didn't come here anymore. There weren't any signs forbidding it so we went inside. I was amazed at the views from the windows. From the kitchen, which appears to be an addition, the view is of the creek and waterfalls which runs across the back yard and down over huge boulders.

I feel so at home here. I went to the town hall and found out who owned the place. I called and talked to the owner. She said it is for sale. She wants more money for it than I can pay but she did say I could go sit there anytime I wanted. Even stay there if I wanted too. She asked me to shut it up for her and check on it whenever I was in New Hampshire. There is no electric, no running water and the outhouse has seen its better days but oh I do feel at home here. Wish I had brought my notebook. I feel a story coming on.....

Had to take one last walk down to the house before we leave for Michigan. Just to say "I will be back" and to take one last listen to the music of the waterfalls.

I brought a note book with me this time. Sitting in this "garden" on this rock is like going to outdoor church. I can feel God here. If God wills it, the owner comes down on the price to where I can manage it, I am going to buy this place to come to in the summers. My new job in Michigan ends in May and begins again in October. This would be the perfect place to come to write and to get closer to God. I could get completely away from the old lifestyle too. If you want to get closer to someone you need to spend time with them and I could spend a lot of time with God here.

∽∽∞∽∽

When I look back at this journal entry, I realize a lot has happened since that day in 1990, and I have had the opportunity to enjoy that space and to learn so much more about God. I was on the right track then and am still on the same track. If you want to get closer to someone you have to spend time with them. Spending time with God is one of the most important things we can do to learn about Him. It is the most important thing I can do in my walk with Him.

When you spend a lot of time with someone you often become more like them. If you have a best friend you find that you like things you didn't know you liked, and you do things you didn't know you could or would do just because they do and it makes them happy. It is the same when you spend time with God.

Who am I? I am the adopted child of God. I have finally found the Father who I missed so much when I was an adolescent youth.

Ephesians 1:3-6

> Blessed be the God and Father of our Lord Jesus Christ, who has blessed us with every spiritual blessing in the heavenly places in Christ, just as He chose us in Him before the foundation of the world, that we would be holy and blameless before Him. In love he predestined us to adoption as the sons (and daughters) through Christ Jesus to Himself, according the kind intention of His will, to the praise of the glory of His grace, which He freely bestowed on us in the Beloved. (NAS)

Ephesians 1:11

> Also we have obtained an inheritance having been predestined according to His purpose who works all things after the counsel of His will. (NAS)

If you are reading this because you want a closer walk with God, you too are one of the CHOSEN ones. Read Romans 8:15-17 and Galatians 4:5-6.

To be adopted means you have been chosen. According to the laws of this land you have to accept the adoption if you are old enough to know about it. The Judge will ask you if you really want to be adopted by this family. All you have to do is say yes.

Because Jesus the Son loves me God the Father loves me. Because God the Father loves me Jesus the Son loves me. I am loved and adopted into the family of God. I am one of the chosen ones. I have accepted the adoption into the family of God.

To accept that you have been chosen by God to be a family member is sometimes hard to comprehend. You can say it and feel joy in it and still not quite understand or believe it. Down deep inside we KNOW we are not good enough. We know that we don't deserve it.

Whenever we depend on ourselves and our actions we fail. We fall down. There is no way we can do enough good works to be worthy of adoption into the family of God. But God says HE predestined us to adoption. He chose us even before the foundation of the world! True, when He created us he gave us free choice. He predestined us to adoption, but we have the choice to say no or yes.

Okay, so first you must realize that Christ actually did die on the cross, and that when He did He took upon Himself ALL the sins of the world. What a load! It is unfathomable that He would and could take on such a load. What a burden He accepted for us. And He did it because His Father asked Him to.

Not just for you and me but all who accept Him as their personal savior. It is not about you or me. It is about Him and what He has done for the world so that we can become Children of God.

He has given us welcome home gifts. They are the gifts of the Holy Spirit and eternal life in our heavenly home. These are the most precious gifts of all. We are welcomed home into the family of God.

In order for me to fully experience the family relationship, I need to be able to accept it.

I am no longer a foster child moved from place to place, but I am truly accepted into the family for no other reason than that God loves me. It isn't about how good I am or what I look like or how much money I can bring. If those things counted I would always be an orphan looking in the window and wishing. No, it is about Him and His unbounding Grace.

It isn't about what I do. All I have to do is believe in who He is and what He did for me. I am who I am because of Him.

I know a couple who have adopted four children. When the oldest was three, they went to the court room to see the judge and complete the adoption. The little boy asked the judge, "Can he really be my daddy now?" The judge said, "Do you want him to be?" He jumped up and ran to his new father and hugged him said, "Yes, he loves me."

Have you accepted the adoption?

If you have, you have been adopted into the family of God. You are a child of God. Nothing or no one can take that away from you. We are brothers and sisters in Christ. Welcome home.

Chapter 4

Praise Him

Psalms 47

> Come everyone. And clap for joy. Shout triumphant praises to the Lord. For the Lord the God above all gods is awesome beyond words. He is the great King of all the earth. (MES)

When I was a child, we went to church twice on Sunday and on Wednesday night every week. Sunday morning was dress up and act like a lady time. Mom would put rag curls in my hair the night before because when I was little my hair was straight as a board. We had to get up early because we had to eat breakfast before we went. We had to take turns in the bathroom getting dressed and brushing our teeth. There were six kids so bathroom time was essential and hard to get as everyone got older.

Early Sunday morning we had Sunday school. We learned all the old stories of the Bible: Noah and the Ark, Jonah and the Whale, Abraham and Isaac, Shadrack, Meshack and Abednego and the Fiery Furnace. Even the adults had Sunday school. When Sunday school was over we had to go to worship service where families all sat together in long pews. We filled up one whole row. I wondered why they called them pews. I thought it was because my brother was sitting there. I remember mom didn't like to sit in the same place all the time, but when Dad was the preacher we had to sit right up front. Boy would we get it after church if we didn't behave. We knew just how far we could push it and were too scared to do more.

The songs on Sunday morning were more somber, and I always wanted the organist to speed it up a bit. The preacher in those days could talk as long as he wanted too. Sometimes it was well past noon before we got to chase our friends around the church yard or head home for Sunday dinner.

Sunday night was a bit more casual. Mom would bring paper and crayons for us if we got bored. The songs were uplifting and peppy, and mom often led the singing. Oh how she loved to sing! The thing I knew was that I loved the praise songs. Whenever I sang them they made me feel like laughing and smiling inside out. They still do that for me. They lift my spirits.

Wednesday was a different story. Wednesday we got to learn stuff. Wednesday was Bible study. We studied the old stories and we memorized verses. There was always a snack afterwards. I was tall and skinny growing like a weed and snacks were always welcome.

We had to practice during the week and got our name on the chart when we knew so many of the verses. "Shoot!" I thought, "Someday I will not need a Bible at all because I will be able to stand right up there and say the whole thing right out loud." That would have been okay except I was too shy to stand up in front of anyone even in that little Bible class. When it was my turn to recite, I would stammer and turn red. If the teacher didn't help me I would just say "The end." I could recite a lot of verses no one ever realized I knew.

Funny thing about those praise songs and Bible verses, they were what kept me going when things went really wrong, and life took me places I really didn't want to be.

Deep within me were those Bible verses. Down in my heart were the songs.

> *I've got the joy, joy, joy, joy down in my heart.*
> *Down in my heart. Down in my heart.*
> *I've got the Joy, joy, joy, joy down in my heart. Down in my heart*
> *to stay.*

> *I've got the love of Jesus, love of Jesus....*

I wonder, how are those little ones going to survive the horrors of this life? Especially when I see so many people who don't send or bring their children to church. And trust me there are horrors in this life. But how are they going to survive without the voice inside that says "Jesus loves me this I know."

Thank God not everyone experiences those really terrible things like rape, abuse or addiction, but they do experience other things. Heart break, betrayal and loss are just a few.

I know that when I got so far down and the only way I could see was up, those verses got me through. Especially the easy ones to remember.

John 3:16

> For God so loved the world that He gave His only Son that whosoever believes in Him will not parish but have eternal life. (NAS)

John 14:1-4

> Let not your heart be troubled. Believe in God believe also in
> Me. In my Father's house are many mansions if it were not so I
> would have told you for I go to prepare a place for you. And if
> I go and prepare a place for you, I will come again and receive
> you to myself that where I am there you may be also. And you
> know the way where I am going. (KJ)

Those verses keep coming back to me and I know who I am. I may not
know why some things happened to me, but I do know who I am and
who my Savior and my Redeemer is.

Journal Entry

February 1991.

*Alone in my room yet again. Thinking why? Why me Lord? Why can't I ever find
someone who really loves me? Why is it that I always think they are the right
one and they turn out to be so wrong? I looked back in this journal I have been
writing in. I didn't do resolutions because I knew I wasn't disciplined enough to
complete them but I did outline some goals I had for myself for the year. My
very first goal had been to find a way to walk closer with Jesus. Yet here I
was having my own little pity party once again.*

*A voice inside me. Deep down where those songs and verses were hidden said.
"You can have the pity party if you really want to but what does it do for you?
I will still be here when you get through but why waste so much time? If you
really want a closer walk with me, all you have to do is hold out your hand. I
haven't gone anywhere." "Listen. If you want joy — sing for it."*

Well I am not sure what that means. Am I so far gone that I think I can sing? NO that was the words to one of those songs! "If you want Joy you can sing for it. If you want Joy you can sing for it, If you want joy you can sing for it. The joy of the Lord is my strength." One of those songs I learned in Sunday school so many many years ago. The Joy of the Lord is my strength! Well I sure need strength.

OKAY LORD. Okay. I got up from my chair and went to the kitchen and filled the sink with water. I started doing the dishes and for some reason before I knew what I was doing I was humming and trying to remember the words to some of those songs.

It has been 10 years since I left the church. I have gone to what I like to call "outside church" on my own. I feel like I don't need people, I can discover God on my own.

It wasn't the first time I walked out on church either. After being abused as a kid and having betrayal and abandonment thrown in for good measure, I still had a heart for God. But I didn't have the lifestyle for a long time. I studied every religion and found them all lacking. I turned by back and walked away. I found friends who didn't ever talk about God. I found that I didn't have to think about it. I could just go have fun and in my heart of hearts I knew right from wrong and I thought I was a pretty good person. I didn't steal or lie or cheat. I kept most of the 10 commandments.

Then I found myself as a single parent raising a child and I felt I needed to teach her about God so I joined the church again. I became an active member doing all I could to make sure my daughter got the right teaching (whatever that was) and made Christian friends. About that time my second marriage didn't just fall apart it blew up. Once again I had failed. Once again I had made a poor choice. I clung to the church and began to work harder. I knew if I could do really good, everything would be okay.

I never do anything half way so I became an active member of a church. I was the youth leader, a Sunday school teacher, and part of the women's group. I was the leader of the junior church. I wasn't really walking closer with God however. It was my do that I was growing not my who.

I married a man who said he loved God as much as I did. He went to church with me for a while and then he felt he didn't really need the ritual of the church.

So when my husband announced one day that he just didn't need to be married anymore and some of the ladies at the church where I had worked so hard turned their backs on me when I needed them, I gave up on church and walked away. I had put my faith in people and church and they had failed me again. I didn't realize until later that you can't put your faith in people and church because even Christians are human. You must put your faith in God and Christ.

So washing dishes and looking out my kitchen window today, I started humming and then singing those praise songs and I found they lifted me up and made me smile. Then I knew it wasn't about the church or the women or even the wild life I had led or the men I had married. It was about God and Christ and the Holy Spirit. It was about praising the name of Jesus. Thanking God for giving His Son. Thanking the Son for taking away all my sins forever. Thanking the Holy Spirit for helping me to see the path back toward the light of God. It wasn't about what I could or did do. None of that mattered. What mattered was what Christ did when He gave up His life for me. What mattered was that God loved me even when no one else did.

⋙⋘

Another step closer.

Lifting up praises to the Lord of Lords.

Loving Him because He first loved me.

Showing my love for Him though songs and praises.

Loving Him as simply as a child.

It is just that simple.

I started reading the Psalms every morning and singing those simple little songs on my way to work. I realized my days were getting better and no matter what was thrown my way I could still be happy. It took some work to get there, but it was so worth it.

Every once in a while I will find myself ready to have a pity party. Then I will do what I told one of my employees to do who had a penchant for degrading and feeling sorry for herself. "When you screw up or make a mistake, go in the back room and set the timer for 5 minutes. You have that long to rant and rage against yourself and when the clock goes off, stop. Come back out with a smile on your face and get back to whatever work you were doing." It works.

In the words of Joyce Meyers "You can be pitiful or powerful but you can't be pitiful and powerful."

As you continue your walk with God find some of those praise songs and sing them every morning and evening. It isn't about the sound of your voice. If you are in a place where you can't sing them out loud, sing them in your head and in your heart.

Get some downloads or CDs of praise music and listen to them when you rise in the morning. Listen to them when you drive your car, when you exercise or walk. People may think you are nuts when they see you talking to yourself at a stop light, but soon they will realize you are just singing at the top of your lungs.

Best of all, lift your hands and praise the Lord. IT FEELS GOOD.

Chapter 5

Why Me Lord?

On my daily walk through the woods, I stop to touch a tree and feel the rough bark and the life coursing through it. I whisper a secret to it. I sit on a rock and look at the tiny flowers. I admire and say good morning to one of those tiny bright orange lizards. I am amazed daily at nature and how it works. I am so excited that God loves His creations so much that He watches over even the tiniest of creatures. They are part of His plan too.

Matthew 6:26

> Consider the birds of the air, they neither sow nor reap or store in barns yet your heavenly Father feeds them. Are you not worth more? (NAS)

Matthew 10:29

> Are not two sparrows sold for a penny yet one does not fall to the ground without your Fathers knowledge. You are worth more than one of these. (NAS)

There is an old song I used to love that has these words; "His eye is on the sparrow and I know He's watching me." If He loves those creatures so much, how much more does He love me?

⚛

Journal Entry

August 1992

I bought it. The Falls House is officially mine. I brought a car load of stuff with me from Michigan and I am moved in and settled. I feel like I have finally come home. Home at the Falls House has its advantages and its disadvantages. I spend most of my time by myself. Cora comes down for coffee and we get together for dinner or help each other with our work sometimes but mostly, I am alone. I am not complaining though. It gives me plenty of time to write and read and be outside sitting on rocks and fixing what I can. There is no electricity and the only running water is in the back yard in the stream. I have a large milk can with a faucet towards the bottom. I painted it black and put it on a platform I made between three trees. I climb up and fill it with water. The sun heats it up and it makes a great shower. I put a blanket around the three trees when I discovered there were hunters across the creek in the woods. This place is so isolated it never crossed my mind that there may be others in the woods. I have to walk a mile and three tenths to get here from the place I park my car. I am here till the end of September. I am finally finding time to write and to be alone with God. Something I have wanted since I decided to go on the quest to get to know Him better.

Sometimes I wonder why I am here and what I am doing. I question myself and my existence. I question my talents and my abilities. Then I think of all I have been blessed with and I feel bad for questioning.

Today I was giving myself a guilt trip for asking "Why me Lord? What have I done to deserve even a few of these blessings? I really make a lot of mistakes and I am no stranger to sin." In the stillness that followed my tirade I heard God's answer. "It's not about you it's about the love." What did He mean? I guess I need to work on that one.

⧓

The very first thing that you need to know is that God loves you unconditionally.

John 3:16

> For God so loved the world that He gave His only begotten Son that whosoever believes in Him shall not perish but have everlasting life.

Let's look at this piece by piece.

For God - because God

God the Father, God the creator, God the Counselor, God the Alpha and Omega, the beginning and the end, the all-knowing, all-seeing, all-being God. It is because

He so loved – loved so much.

It is hard to imagine the kind of love God has for us. I think of the love of a parent who looks at a new baby for the first time and their heart swells with the fullness of it all. I think of the deep joy two people feel who have been through the fire in their marriage and come out the other side of those trials walking together as one. I think of the compassionate love of those who willingly give up their own comfort to help the destitute children and homeless peoples of the world. That is love, but those kinds of love are mere drops in the sea of love that God has for His own. I think we could write a book or many books on God's love, and it would not cover how God feels about His creation.

The World – the whole world –

Pretty generic isn't it? It means everyone and everything on the earth. The WHOLE world. It doesn't matter what your color is, where you are from or why you live and do what you do. Nothing you can do matters in the shadow of this love. He doesn't say if you do this or that He will love you. He says HE LOVED. We can't change His love. We can't deserve His love. We can't win His love. We can never be worthy of His love. He doesn't ask us to. His love is not based on us or anyone or anything in the world. He loves us because He created us. God loves His creation so much.

That He Gave – Because He loved the world He gave us a gift. –

God's part of the deal. God gave. That's it. We don't deserve a gift. We didn't earn a gift. We aren't that special. We are just a speck in the whole scheme of things. But God gave.

When you give a gift to someone, often it is because they have done something to deserve it. Maybe they got another year older or they did something nice and you want to say thank you. Perhaps it is an anniversary or they are ill, and you want to make them feel a little better if you can. When you give the gift you are letting go of it and hoping they like it. You can't control what they do with your gift. It could go into the back of the closet or out on the table for everyone to see. It could be given to someone else. After you give the gift you have to accept the thanks and walk away. God's gift is different. It is more than we could ever imagine yet God gave us free will. It is our choice whether to accept His gift or not, and what we do with it.

His only (begotten) Son – The Son He begot. His only one. – The Gift.

Have you ever spent hours writing a story, painting a picture, making music or sewing? Perhaps you have spent hours picking out just the right gift for someone you care about. When you are done you have a feeling of elation. You want to say "Look everyone, look what I have done." You want that gift to be the most important gift that person has received. You love it so much you almost want to keep it for yourself. You are nervous about whether the recipient will like it even a little bit. You know they can never really love it like you do.

Whenever I write a story, it takes me often as much as thirty hours to prepare it to tell. It can be funny, serious, sad or happy, fantasy or real life. None of that matters. What matters is that I am working hard to tie it up in its package and put a beautiful bow on it. I am usually thinking of the people I am going to give this story to. I want them to like it. I want them to love it as much as I do. I want them to take it home with them. I want it to make a difference in their lives somehow. Perhaps the laughter that comes with it will chase away a tear or lighten a load a little bit. Perhaps the depth of the story will touch a part of their heart and lead them to think more clearly about some area of their life. Maybe listening to someone else's imagined story will give them pause and help them to re-imagine theirs.

If I put that much thought into a story, and if you put that much thought into your gifts, how much more has God put into the greatest gift of all--**HIS SON**

That whosoever –

Are you a whosoever? I am. Anyone can be a whosoever. Anyone can decide that they will accept the gift. When you bring a gift to someone and they feel they don't deserve it, they sometimes say, "Oh no thanks. I don't deserve that. I didn't earn it." You say, "That's okay. It is a gift. You don't need to earn it."

No one can out-give God. He gave us His only Son. He doesn't expect us to earn His gift. All we have to do is accept His gift. All we have to do is be a whosoever.

Believes –

Whoops now here is our part. Yes we have a part to play, a job to do to become a whosoever. It is to believe. Now you say, "Oh that's easy." Wait it isn't as easy as it sounds. We have to believe in something we cannot see. We have to believe that even though we don't deserve it or earn it He loves us enough to give us this gift. We have to believe it in spite of all the lies the enemy (the father of lies) tells us about our worthlessness. We have to believe despite all the science, technology, and experts that say there is no God. We have to believe that the God others say does not exist gave us His Son to die in our place. We have to believe that He loves us that much. We have to believe that the Son loves the Father and us so much that He would die for us. All we need to do is to believe.

In Him – His only begotten Son.

That is who we are to believe in. God's Son. We can read the Bible and know the stories of the one they call Jesus. We can hear of His birth at Christmas time and His death and resurrection at Easter. We can sing the songs and color the Easter Eggs. But do we really deep down inside KNOW that Jesus is the Christ, the Son of the Living God? Do we know it is for US he died? Do we take it personal? Do we know that when the Father looks at us He sees the beauty of His Son? Do we know we look like Christ? Do we accept the fact that we are now adopted into the family of God? Do we realize when God looks at us there is a family resemblance? Do we know how beautiful we are in the eyes of God? Do we really believe?

Shall not perish - Perish – to become ruined, spoiled or destroyed.

Believers shall NOT perish. Shall not be ruined, spoiled or destroyed. The Bible calls Satan the great destroyer. It says he comes only to steal, kill and destroy. But we shall not perish. We shall not be destroyed. That too is part of God's gift. He gave His Son to die in our place. When He looks at us He sees His Sons and Daughters clean and beautiful. Because of the gift of His Son we shall not perish.

But will have everlasting life – The promise is everlasting life.

Life eternal lasting forever with God as Father. How great is that? To live always with God as Father, to inherit His kingdom, to walk in the kingdom of God always in His presence. To be seated at the table with the rest of His family and to know that we belong. We have a part in the Father and He has a part in us.

God has already done His part now it depends on us. We have to believe. We merely have to accept the gift of His Son. This is His plan. We could not see how anyone could give a gift so precious to ones such as us. But wait! He created us. He loved us even before he created us. He loved us when we were an idea, a thought. He spoke us into creation, and He gave us the free will to make the choice. We have the right to an inheritance from our Father, the Lord of all creation. He will teach us lessons, give us gifts, fill us with His Spirit, He sometimes corrects us and He always loves us. He loves us more than any human ever could. When we are hurt or disillusioned we can crawl upon His lap. He will hold us until we can walk again side by side with Him.

Knowing and accepting His unconditional love is another step in taking that closer walk with Him.

In my journal entry today twenty-three years later, I wrote about God's unconditional love. I am still discovering how great that love is. I will probably be still in awe of it when I meet Him face to face.

Chapter 6

Prayer

Another step on the path toward a closer walk with God is learning to communicate with Him. Without communication a relationship does not exist. It is one thing to say I am a child of God, it is another thing to actually have a one- on-one relationship with the Father. How can you really get to know anyone without ever talking to them? You can read about Him and hear other people talk about Him, but if you don't talk directly to Him you may never have the opportunity to get to know Him personally. We do that through praise and prayer. God loves to have us tell Him our problems and thank Him for his blessings. He loves to hear from His children the same as we love to hear from our own children.

Strong's Bible Dictionary describes prayer as:

Pray – implore, beg, intercede, to ask, to ponder or muse aloud, to petition, to interrogate, to request, to wish for, to call, to invite, to supplicate

Prayer – incantation, intercede in prayer, uttered contemplation, request, wish petition, to supplicate

Webster's New Riverside Dictionary says this:

Pray – To address God or a deity especially with devout petition. To request something fervently. To implore.

Prayer – An expression especially of devout petition addressed to God or a deity. A formal set of words used in praying. An earnest entreaty.

Journal Entry

March 18, 1993

Well here I am a Grandmother again. This is the 4th one and this time I did not get to go to the hospital with Lesa. I stayed with the other kids. Lesa came home within hours after my 3rd grandson was born. What a bundle of joy this special little boy is. Lesa was sick throughout this whole pregnancy. I came often after work and helped her with the kids and the house and dinner and the like. I was pretty worried about her for a while. I spent a lot of time on my knees. Sometimes I don't even know how to pray for her or her family.

Teach me Lord to Pray, Teach me Lord to Pray, Teach me Lord to Pray, Thy will be done.

May thy will be done, may thy will be done, may thy will be done, be done in me.

The words to an old Sunday school song from my youth. I didn't really think about it much before now.

I am really looking forward to going to the Falls House in NH in May when my job for the city ends for the summer. It doesn't pick back up again until the first of October. I am not sure how long I will get to stay. I hate to leave Lesa and the kids but I do need a break. I need a break from work and my life here. I find myself like Paul who asks Why do I want to do what I know I should but end up doing what I know I shouldn't do? I have been staying at Marian's. Renting a room from her. My stuff is all stored here and there. I will be taking a car load of things out to the Falls House soon. I think one of my friends will be going with me.

Journal Entry

May 1993,

We went to the Falls House for a week. Took a load of stuff out.

It was fun and funny at the same time. My friend loves the place, but does not really love no running water and the outdoor shower and outhouse. She talked most of the way out the first day even to the point of reading all the road signs out loud. I started singing the next day I sang all the songs I could remember and didn't stop till I got to Teddy Bears Picnic. Then she called a halt to it. I laughed. I know I can't carry a tune in a bucket. Then she got to reading signs again and I started singing. We both got to laughing until it was all okay. Funny how some people just don't know they don't have to talk to fill the silence until something wakes them up like that. We actually had a great time. She asked me some questions about my belief in God and stuff. I answered the best I knew how. Not sure if it was enough.

I do know my life style does not always say "Christian" although I have a deeply spiritual love for God and Christ. I know He has seen me through some very hard times. I also know I cannot put my trust in all Christians and church. I have to put my trust in God and not people.

I have often found myself on my knees praying when things are really down and I am feeling so alone. At the Falls House I find myself praying about all kinds of things. Like saying thanks for all of this. I feel here as I do when I walk in those woods in Michigan that I take care of for another friend when he is in Virginia. There I feel the connection with God and nature but here I feel it even more. I will be back for the summer in a couple of weeks. Looks like it is coming up to evaluation time. Time to re- evaluate the life I lead and how I am going to fulfill my goal to walk closer to God. What do I have to give up to do so and what friendships I can retain. I guess I need to pray about that too. Prayer, another step closer in my walk with God.

When I look back on these journal entries, I can see how far I have come in my walk with God. I know that prayer was a big part of that journey and it helped me on my way more than I even realized. Nowadays my feet don't hit the floor without my saying either in my heart or out loud, "Thank you God for another day and for guiding me and loving me."

Prayer is a two way street. It is communication. It opens the channels to give us a line to the heavenly Father, and it also gives the Father an open heart to respond to. He likes nothing better than to love us and know that we love Him.

It is during that first thought of the morning that I often hear him clearly. Today He brought to my mind the name and situation of an elderly woman at church. I am not sure what I am supposed to do for her, so I asked Him to show me a way to bring a blessing to her. While I was doing that the name of another elderly woman who is not from the church I attend came to mind too. I have been thinking of her for a couple of days. I will give her a call later today when I know she is up. She has been through a tough time lately, and I know she can use some encouragement and friendship. Perhaps I will ask her to go to lunch with me sometime this week.

I rise early and love that time between dark and dawn. The time when the whole earth seems to take a deep breath and pause just for a moment. Then all of creation becomes the dawn chorus and begins to sing its praises to the Creator. It is a holy time for me, a time to worship and give thanks, a time to pray.

I love that line of open communication. I want to keep that line open. I don't want to disconnect even in my sleep.

Did you know there are 650 prayers listed in the Bible? There are approximately 450 recorded answers to prayers in the Bible.

Prayer is initiated by God in Genesis 3:8-13 and Genesis 4:9 and it is first initiated by man in Genesis 4:26.

In Matthew 6:14-15 and also in Luke 11:1-4, the apostles ask Jesus how to pray. He uses the prayer we call the Lord's Prayer as an example to teach them. I think they ask Him because they saw that He communicated with His Father that way. They saw the power of prayer and the miracles that Jesus performed with prayer.

The ministry of Jesus was surrounded by prayer. He prayed from the beginning to the end. He always found time for prayer. Often He went off by Himself somewhere to pray. Sometimes He was too busy to eat or sleep, but He never was too busy to pray. He even prayed just before He gave up His spirit asking His Father to forgive those who had done this terrible crucifixion to Him.

God answers prayers. I know because time after time when I could see no other way I went to God and He answered. I know because He has provided for my needs in many ways. I know because I have seen the healings and the blessings first hand.

I set aside time each morning right when I first get up and as soon as I have no distractions. I also pray at other times during the day and end each day with a prayer at night. In Daniel 6:10 Daniel set aside times each day so regularly you could probably set your watch by him.

Find a place to pray. Jesus climbed a mountain to pray or went into a garden. I have a chair in the corner of the living room where I can watch the sun rise and pray. Sometimes when I am traveling, when I am with other people for a conference, or am teaching it is hard to find that quiet space. I have gone into the bathroom or the shower to find that few minutes alone with God.

Pray out loud when you can. I often find myself talking to God throughout the day, in the car or at other times when I am alone. It opens the lines of communications and makes talking to God your Father seem more coherent and conversational. Try praying out loud.

Use a prayer list. Thanks to my younger sister Cora for sharing her idea, I now keep a piece of paper with names or thoughts on it in my pocket. I call it my prayer pocket. When I stick my hand into my pocket I feel that piece of paper and remember to say a prayer for those people or that idea.

Write down your list each day. Keep it brief. Add to it as necessary. Keep it where you can see it often. These are the people and thoughts you are holding up to the Father throughout the day.

Journal your thoughts and ideas about prayer and your results. Do you feel closer to God as you talk to Him? Remember He is your Father and you can talk with Him more easily than you can an earthly father. He already knows everything about you, so you don't have to worry about shocking Him or surprising Him. With Him there are no surprises.

During my private prayer time there is a formula that I use.

First I open with praise. There are many praises in the Word. Psalms is especially full of them. Psalm 18 declares "I love you, O Lord, my strength. The Lord is my rock, my fortress and my deliverer. My God is my rock in whom I take refuge. He is my shield and the hope of my salvation…"

Psalm 19 is one of my favorites. It begins "The heavens declare the glory of God. The skies proclaim the work of His hands. Day after day they pour forth speech, night after night they display knowledge…" and ends "May the words of my mouth and the meditation of my heart be pleasing in your sight O Lord my Rock and my Redeemer". The whole of Psalm 19 is truly a prayer of praise and worship by David.

Next I ask forgiveness for my sins and short comings. This is also in Psalms 19:12. God already knows what these sins are and has already forgiven me but He wants me to ask Him anyway acknowledging what He has done for me. Sometimes the things in my heart bring tears to my eyes and breaks me because I am not perfect. I know it but I also know I am forgiven. His forgiving love for me makes me know it is not my "worthiness" but His love that brings me back to Him. I ask His help in learning to forgive others because I know unforgiveness carried around in my heart makes static on the communication lines and sometimes even drops the call. Above all I want to keep those lines between my Father and myself open.

Then I talk to Him about my day, my life and the people in it. I ask His help and guidance in all I do. I ask for Him to provide all my needs. I ask for His hand on the people I love and those on my "list".

Finally I sit silent in His presence. He already knows my needs, He already has provided for me. Now I just listen. Sometimes, I hear that still small voice inside my spirit that gives me the answers I have been seeking. Other times it is a shout that wakes me out of my reverie and says "JUST DO IT LAURETTA" or "WRITE IT". Other times there is just the silence. That peaceful place where time stands still and I know I am in His presence and His glory surrounds me. I am safe here on His lap and in His arms.

CHAPTER 7

Forgiveness

The enemy sets up road blocks designed to keep us from having a closer walk with God. One of those road blocks is unforgiveness. Christ speaks of it in many places. He even addresses it in the Lord's Prayer. "Forgive us as we forgive others."

I have been a Christian for a long time. I understand that God forgives us when we do wrong. We are not perfect. I am not perfect that is for sure. But then, if we were perfect would we need God? Would we even be here or would we be back home with the Father?

All those times that I studied and learned Bible verses and sang praise songs when I was in Sunday school held me in good stead as an adolescent and young adult. I never understood the why of all that happened or the way it all came about, but I did know through it all that God was there for me. Knowing Him was keeping me sane and able to carry on, to love and trust people. Knowing Him was giving me hope and teaching me to forgive.

⚬⚬⚬

Journal Entry

August 1994,

Didn't get here to the Falls House until late this year. My job changed again and it is already August. It is a hot one today but I can still hear the water running in the creek behind the house. Running down, down, down past the back yard to the drop that makes the water falls under the kitchen window. You can hear that water no matter what the season. Spring the falls are so loud you can hear it from any part of the property. Winter, summer and fall it varies day by day but it always sings me to sleep at night.

It is a hard day. I have something to do that is not pleasing. I am not sure how I am going to manage it all. I realized when I got the news that one of the men from my childhood had passed away, that I still had not really forgiven all those people in my life who really hurt me. I thought I had. I worked through my anger and my hurt with my dad and sat by his bedside for 16 nights when he died. I thought that all of that was gone but when I got the news of this passing, the feelings I had were not of sadness or care. All those feelings of disgust and anger and hatred came flooding back and all I wanted to do was say "Good."

I know I need to spend time here by myself dealing with all this. Letting those feelings go. When I even think about it all, I just want to shut down and go away somewhere safe. A counselor I had when Mark and I were getting a divorce said one thing that made a difference in my life. It was probably the only thing he said or did that helped. He said "You bury your stuff deep inside and pretend it doesn't matter. When you take garbage out and bury it in the ground and tamp it down tight, it just stays garbage. When you dig it up it is still garbage. But if you spread it around on top of the ground where the wind and rain and sun can heat it up and wash it clean, it becomes fertilizer for good things to grow."

Today, I gave that some thought and I started taking the things that bothered me or hurt me and pretending they were garbage. I would visualize taking it outdoors and spreading it around on top of the flower beds or the vegetable garden and letting nature take its course.

Whew, thank God I have a heavenly Father that knows and understands because I surely don't know how to do this by myself. Thank God I have space where I can let it all out and give it all to God.

I know all those Bible verses I learned and all those songs I learned as a child had a big impact on how I responded to what life had in store for me.

When I think about what life has in store for so many of us and I see so many that don't know or acknowledge God I wonder "How can they learn to forgive and love again?"

My goodness I was in my 30s before I actually dealt with forgiving my dad and here I am almost 20 years later and some of these old garbage things still pop up. I guess you have to take each person and individual thing separate and forgive them one at a time.

That is a different concept. I thought God just covered all your sins and washed them away in one big lump. Perhaps Christ suffered for each one of them! Whew, now that is horror.

One thing I have learned about forgiveness is that it is much easier to forgive or say you forgive than it is to forget the past. Forgiveness begins with God and ends with you.

Mica 7:18

> Who is a God like you, who pardons sin and forgives the transgression of the remnant of his inheritance? You do not stay angry forever but delight to show mercy. (NIV)

Mica 7:19

> You will again have compassion on us; you will tread our sins underfoot and hurl all our iniquities into the depths of the sea. (NIV)

How do you forgive others and not hold onto the hurt?

The enemy reminds us of the things we have done or the things that has been done to us to get us going again in the wrong direction when he sees we are taking God's hand and letting Him lead.

You can't forgive everything at once. You have to take it one step at a time, especially if you have a lot to forgive.

Mark 11:25

> And when you stand praying and you have anything against anyone, forgive him so your father in heaven may forgive you. (NIV)

Colossians 1:13-14

> For he has rescued us from the kingdom of darkness and brought us into the kingdom of the Son whom he loves in whom we have redemption the forgiveness of sins. (NIV)

Every once in a while you will be reminded of something. Take that thought, pull it out and look at it and say "Okay that did happen, I forgive it." Every time it comes up all you need to do is say "Oh that is already forgiven." and soon it will be gone. What is out in the light can't hurt you. It is what you keep hidden in the dark that has such harmful power.

Oh and yes, you have to forgive yourself too.

First you call whatever it is exactly what it is. If it is a lie that hurt you, you call it a lie. You can't say, "I forgive that little falsehood or that story." You have to call things as they are.

Then you have to accept the responsibility for it. If you did it say you did it. If it was done to you, then say it was done to you. If you are feeling guilty about it STOP THAT! It doesn't come from God.

Psalm 103:12

> As far as the east is from the west, so far has He removed our transgressions from us. (NIV)

God took all our guilt away. The enemy is the one who is constantly bringing our faults and wrong doings up to God and condemning us. God does not pay attention to that. It says Jesus took our sins and paid the price for them. We are declared not guilty by reason of substitution.

I John 1:9

> If we confess our sins, he is faithful and just and will forgive us our sins and purify us from all unrighteousness. (NIV)

In my solitude, I get on my knees and beg forgiveness. God has already forgiven me. I know that He wants me to ask forgiveness for each of my sins.

Sometimes I catch myself doing something and that little voice inside says STOP THAT! The closer your walk is with God the more often that will happen to you. I call it the Holy Spirit nudge. Sometimes when I am just not paying attention He reaches out and smacks me one. That is what I call a God wake-up call.

My mouth gets me into all kinds of trouble. I say things one way and mean another. I blurt out what is on my mind. I often hear myself say something that does not sound like it came from the mouth of a woman of God. I am like Paul who questions why is it that I want to do the right thing but I end up doing the wrong thing. In that case all you can do is ask for forgiveness and pray that God will help you control this thing.

I have to remind myself of the last verse of Psalms 19 – "Let the words of my mouth and the meditations of my heart be acceptable unto you Lord." (NIV)

There are many scriptures pertaining to forgiveness. Look up forgiveness in your concordance and check out the verses. Find ones that resonate with you and put them on 3x5 cards to look at often.

Think of the things and people you need to forgive. Do it as they come to mind, don't dwell on what they have done. Hold it up to God and ask forgiveness for them and for yourself. Then say out loud "I forgive this …….(deed) I forgive this……..(person). Sit with it for a while.

Whenever the enemy brings up something you have done or reminds you of something done to you, send him packing. Give it back to God.

Ask God for forgiveness daily or whenever you catch yourself doing something or saying something you regret. Don't sleep on it or wait. Do it right then. You don't want to put it in a bag and carry it around. That can get pretty heavy after a while.

CHAPTER 8

Fear

Jesus said, "Fear not for I am with you always, even unto the ends of the Earth." Fear is addressed in many locations in the Bible. David was afraid for his life when Saul was after him. He was often fearful but he took his fear to God.

An acronym for Fear is False Evidence Appearing Real.

Fear is the opposite of faith. It is the enemy's way of attacking us from within.

⸎

Journal Entry

September 1994

Yesterday a young couple came into the Falls House. They were so intent on each other that they did not even notice I was there. They came in and sat down on the sofa and started hugging and kissing.

I cleared my throat and said "Well hello!" They jumped and I could see on their faces the internal conflict between the responses of flight or fight.

When they looked up, there I was sitting right across from them! I could have been a ghost by the look of them.

The girl stammered "We didn't know you were here!" Well that was obvious. I said "This is my home, do you just walk into someone's home and use it when you think they are not home?" She seemed offended and said "Well, we didn't know you were here!"

I think they didn't get it. I think I need a dog. I did not hear them coming. Anyone could come in on me with no warning! It started a little nagging fear in my mind.

Alone in a remote cabin in the woods! I hadn't thought of it that way before. I hadn't thought about "People". I am cautious of the bears and moose that go through the yard. I am careful of the spiders and snakes that claim a portion of this place but I never thought to be wary of people. Everyone around here seems to be really nice. I have met all my neighbors, even those down below. They all know I am here and that I plan on staying....

I didn't sleep well last night. I woke to all the night sounds. The old night mares came thundering back into my head and imagination.

I thought about the note I found recently in my Bible from the man who owns the property across the creek. It wasn't scary at the time, but thinking about it now, I realize he had to come in the house when I was gone even though I had the place locked up.

I guess I better go to the hardware store today and get some new locks so I can batten down the hatches at night when I go to bed. And yes, I am going to get a dog! At least a dog will hear people coming and warn me.

Man what is this fear thing? I haven't had those nightmares for a long time! I thought they were gone.

$$\iff$$

Fear is the opposite of faith. It is the enemy's way of attacking us from within, for putting thoughts in our mind, and shaking our faith. I could have let this fear drive me away from the Falls House and let it block my path to a closer walk with God. I almost did.

It took a few days before I realized actually what was beginning to happen. Then I just got right down on my knees. First I asked for forgiveness for not trusting Him. Then I asked for protection and help in tossing those fears right out the front door. I actually visualized doing it.

Fear can limit how we function in this world. It can cause health issues, it can change our behavior, and limit our possibilities.

Fear is not from God. Fear is the opposite of faith.

God said, "Fear not for I am with you always even unto the end of the Earth."

He is not telling us not to feel fear rather He is telling us not to live in that fear and hold onto it. He is saying trust Him to take care of us.

David hid from Saul in fear.

He asked God to protect Him and He did.

Ephesians 6:13-17

> "Therefore, take up the full armor of God, so that you will be able to resist in the evil day, and having done everything, to stand firm. Stand firm therefore, having girded your loins with truth and having put on the breastplate of righteousness, and having shod your feet with the preparation of the gospel of peace. In addition to all, taking up the shield of faith with which you will be able to extinguish all the flaming arrows of the evil one. And take the helmet of salvation and the sword of the Spirit which is the Word of God." (NAS)

The shield of faith and the breast plate of righteousness covers our hearts. The helmet of salvation covers our head and protects our mind from those fearful thoughts. Imagine yourself putting on that helmet. Take it in your hands, put it on your head. Arrange your hair around it. Adjust the chin strap. Protect your mind. Change your thoughts. Do not let fear run your life or your mind. Fill your heart and mind with the faith that God will take care of you, that He will see you through whatever it is that is coming against you.

CHAPTER 9

Study His Word

I start my day out every day that I can with God's Word. This quiet time in the morning is so important to me that when I miss it, my whole day feels as though something is lacking.

I start by praying for wisdom, enlightenment and understanding. If I only have a few minutes, I pick a scripture that I can meditate on every chance I get during the day. Sometimes it is a Psalm. So many of the Psalms are praise and worship Psalms.

I didn't always start my day this way. I used to read when I could find the time, study when I had a particular thing I wanted to know or when I was writing a story or an essay. Sometimes a friend or my daughter and I would decide we wanted to study His Word. It was hit or miss. More often than not it was a miss.

Journal entry

August 1995,

Back at the Falls House finally. Got here late again this year. Only this time it is to stay. Well, maybe till winter that is. My job transferred me to a bookstore in New Hampshire. I spent most of last winter here at the camp until I went to back to Michigan to work the end of February. I won't be staying here for the winter. I have nothing to prove. It was very cold here last year. The house is not insulated very well and you can feel the cold though the windows. I have to get busy and fix some boards around under the house so the wind and critters don't just blow through. I will put some insulation on the big doors and hang up plastic over the door and windows.

I never got warm last year. I would be up every two hours to stoke the fire. I would sleep in as many clothes as I could. I would get up and hurry to get washed and dressed so I could walk the mile and a half to the car which was cold. I would drive the few miles to work in a cold store that didn't get warm until at least ten in the morning. Then I would get back in the cold car, drive to the parking place, and walk back to the house. It would take about four hours before I could get it warm enough to take off my heavy coat. Nope, I don't have anything to prove. Not planning on doing that again.

There were some positives to this time though. I spent a lot of time talking with God and I spent a lot of time writing stories. I also spent a fair amount of time in the woods. I learned a lot about the creatures that live here and share my space.

One morning when I was walking out on snow shoes and it was just getting day light, I had the feeling that I was being watched. The woods were silent. I could hear my own breath and the crunch of my snowshoes on the crusted snow. I just kept walking. Then I came to the curve in the trail and I stopped and slowly turned back to see what was stalking me. It was a bob cat. He was beautiful. I did not feel threatened by him at all. He was walking in my tracks. He stopped when I stopped. He followed in my footsteps all the way to the head of the trail by the bridge and then he went off into the woods up by the pond. Looking for food I suppose.

I suppose thinking about the cold makes it feel cooler today. It sure is some kind of hot here this summer.

I am going to run an ad for a house sitting position this fall. Probably next month. I will want to get moved in before freeze up. I am asking God to give me the grace to know where the place is for me.

Been writing a lot since I got here. Wouldn't have thought I would have the time taking on a new store and the like but this place is such a creative place. I can't seem to sit without a pen and some paper.

I have a lot of questions about what I am here for and what I am supposed to be doing. It is in His Word that we find the answers to life's questions. When I asked Him what to do, He told me to study His word.

⬦

When God said to study His Word, He didn't mean just to read through the Bible. Yes, the Bible is God's Word and it is inspired, but He meant to study His word.

How do you go about that? Before you begin each session of study, pray for guidance and wisdom.

There are lots of ways to study God's word. In the interest of this book I will explain three of them. There are some things that you will need before beginning either of these methods:

1. Get a Bible you feel comfortable with. There are many versions of the Bible. They range from the old *King James Version* to the *The Message Bible.* There are study Bibles with notes. There are comparative Bibles that give you two or three versions side

by side. I suggest you use the one you find easy to read and understand, and that you also have an older version such as the *New King James* or the *New International Version*. That way if you find it difficult to understand what the author is trying to say, you will have another reference point. If that is not feasible, just use the one that you feel most comfortable with. You can get either a bound copy or an electronic copy. I prefer a Bible I can hold in my hand and turn the pages and highlight passages, so I prefer the bound copy.

2. Get a good Bible dictionary. There are quite a few on the shelves at your local Bible bookstore. I suggest *Strong's Complete Dictionary of Bible Words*. Strong's is divided up by Greek, Hebrew and English. I also have one called *Smith's Bible Dictionary*.

3. Get a Bible concordance. It is very helpful. It will help you find references throughout the Bible on whatever subject you are studying. *Strong's Concordance* is very complete. There are also many others out there. I suggest you check them out and decide which one you want to work with.

4. Get a journal and a notebook. The journal is to record your thoughts about what you have read. The notebook to write down your questions and make notes about words you look up and, the other locations in the Bible that cover a particular topic. You could also use your electronic note book or iPad.

Pick your study time carefully so as to avoid as many distractions as possible. I chose early morning right after I feel rested, when it is quiet in the house, and I can minimize the distractions. A lot of people don't get up as early as I do, so that eliminates a lot of phone calls.

You will find all kinds of distractions. Your husband or kids or the dog will want something. The neighbors will call. The phone will ring. Stay with it. Put a do not disturb sign on your door. Shut the phone off. Tell the family you are busy and will not be available during that time.

One thing I had learned about meditation and study was that the mind will wander. You just need to bring it back gently and sit in the quiet again. Each time you do that you win a little of the battle. It is a battle. The enemy will tell you all kinds of things to make you think or do something else. He does not want you communicating with God. He does not want you to find a close relationship with the Father, and he knows studying the word will help bring you closer to Him.

There are always some distractions, and most of them are from my own making. I shut the cell phone off, but forget to shut off the house phone; I start a load of wash and it gets off balance; the timer on the oven goes off or the power flickers causing the smoke alarm and carbon monoxide detectors to buzz. I just shut them off and then bring myself back to the place I was. I close my eyes and ask again for guidance and understanding.

Plan 1. Read Through the Bible

1. Begin at the beginning of both the Old Testament and the New Testament. You can do one chapter a day from each. If you do that you will be finished with the New Testament before you finish the Old Testament. You can either add more chapters each day of the Old Testament or read the New Testament again. I vote for the later. Re-reading the New Testament will only add to your knowledge and understanding of God.
2. Map out your reading plan. Use a calendar and mark off each date that you set aside time to study.
3. Decide what is the best way for you to learn. Do you learn best by listening, by reading or by writing it down?

a. If listening is your best way, get a copy of the Bible on CD or MP3. Make sure it is a voice you can easily listen to and one that does not put you to sleep.

b. If reading works best, you can use whichever mode of reading you chose, a bound book or electronic one. I prefer to hold the book in my hand. I use a highlighter while I read. I underline or highlight the parts that make me think or hit home to me.

c. If writing helps read the passage, then write down your thoughts and questions. If it is a verse you want to memorize, write the verse in you notebook and also on a 3x5 card to carry with you.

4. Use your journal to record your progress; and use your notebook to keep notes and questions in.

I remember when I decided to read the Bible all the way through in a year. I got one of those planers that tell you just what you are supposed to read and when to read it. You can get them from your church, on-line or at a Bible bookstore.

I never got through it though. I have read the bible all the way through a number of times, but when I tried to use a planner, I was not successful. There is nothing wrong with using one if you can follow it. It helps keep you on track. Although it didn't work for me it might for you. Do what works best for you.

The problem I have with using a planner is I tend to get interested and read beyond the assigned passage. I want to know what is going on. The Bible has some really good stories in it. As a storyteller, I am more interested in the stories then in following a plan. When I got off track I felt guilty and that makes studying and reading the bible a chore not a joy. God doesn't want us to feel guilty. When we do, it puts a block in the way of our learning.

The Old Testament is history, law and prophecy. It is important to study it to find out where we came from, and why or how we got the way we are. It gives directions on how the Israelites were to live and worship God. It also tells us much about Christ and His birth, death and resurrection. It gives us stories that help us to teach our children morals.

The New Testament tells the life story of Christ. It gives us directions on how we as followers of Christ are supposed to live. It tells us who Christ is, and who we are in Christ.

For every question you have, there is an answer in the Bible. As Solomon said, "There is nothing new under the sun." It has all been thought of or done before, just in different times and context.

Plan 2. Study the Bible by topic of interest.

1. Study the Bible by Subject.
2. Use your concordance to find everything in the Bible on a certain word or topic.
3. Use your Bible dictionary to help make the meanings clear.
4. Find all the references in the Bible that refer to a particular topic.
5. Ask yourself this list of questions:

   a. Why am I interested in this?
   b. What does it mean to me?
   c. What kind of impact does it have on my life at the present?
   d. What kind of impact will it have in the future?
   e. How will I use this information in my daily life?

    f. What does it tell me about God the Father, The Son, and The Holy Ghost?

    g. How does it help me to get to know them better?

    h. What other questions you can think of that would be relevant to this particular study?

6. Find a couple of books on the topic. Ask your pastor or friends from church to recommend books on the subject.

7. Use your journal to record your progress. Use your notebook to write down what you learned, where to find out more on the subject, and questions you need to ask about it.

For a while I stumbled around in the Bible and read some here and some there. Then one day I was thinking about a subject I wanted to know more about. I have a good concordance, and I looked the subject up. Then I decided to copy the page out of it, go to each scripture, and study what it said about that subject. It was difficult to understand just what was meant by some of it, so I went to the Bible bookstore and looked for books on the subject. I discovered that there were a lot of different opinions on the subject and on the scriptures that talked about it.

What was I supposed to believe? What was I supposed to do? I recognized some of the authors, so I started with them. What a diverse group of believers they were!

I went back to the scriptures and read them again. Some of them didn't seem to really fit with the question I was asking. I put them aside. I looked at the ones that did seem to fit.

Then I sat with them on my lap during my quiet time and asked God for guidance on this particular subject. In the end, if you remember as the Bible tells us "be still and know" God will give you what is the best answer for you.

You will find that one day someone is having a problem and a scripture will jump into your head. You will remember something that will help them.

In studying God's Word you will get to know more about God. You will understand more, what it means to say, "Abba, Father". While sitting in the quiet and contemplating His word, you will find answers to questions you thought were unanswerable.

Plan 3. Join a Bible study group

Join an existing Bible study group or get together with friends and begin your own.

Your group can decide to use a study guide, or you can decide to read and discuss one of the books from the Bible.

There are a lot of study guides available on topics or books of the Bible. Your group should decide which one they want to use. Everyone should have a copy of the book or study guide.

1. Open each group session with prayer asking God to lead your study.
2. Have one person in your group who is knowledgeable about what you are studying and can lead the sessions in the right direction.
3. Be open to everyone's ideas or thoughts without being judgmental or critical.

4. Use a concordance to look up other verses in the Bible that coincide with the study.

5. Ask someone to address the group on this topic, or find other books on the topic that you can share with the group over the course of the study.

6. Make a list of questions that each of you would like to have answered by this study.

7. Answer the questions posed in the study guide.

8. Study the next chapter before coming to the next session so you can be prepared with questions and thoughts about it.

9. Use your journal to record your progress and your notebook to write down what you learned, where to find out more on the subject and questions you need to ask.

10. Close your session with a period of meditation and prayer.
    Please remember these are only suggestions. There are lots of way to study God's word.

CHAPTER 10

Faith

Strong's Bible Dictionary says the English translation of the word faith means "trustworthiness, fidelity, steadiness, expectation, hope, full confidence, belief, to be firm, steady and true, certainty and reliable."

In the Hebrew language it means "believe or truth."

In Greek "confidence and hope in – to anticipate usually with pleasure-credence, conviction, truth or the truthfulness of God or a religious teacher, reliance upon Christ for salvation, constancy, truth itself, assurance."

Matthew 8:10 tells the story of the Roman centurion who came to Jesus because his servant was ill. He believed that all Jesus had to do was say the word and his servant would be well even though he was miles away. Because of his great faith it happened just as he asked. Jesus was amazed at his faith.

Matthew 9:22 is the story of a woman who was healed from an issue of blood by touching Jesus robe. It was not the robe which made her well but her faith.

In my journals there are countless entries where faith plays a big role in my life. Some of them are simple little tales of need. Some are horrendous stories of illness, healing and hope. Some are very funny stories too. God does have a sense of humor.

Here is one that might lighten your day a little as you take your walk.

❦

Journal Entry

May 1996

I was feeling desperate as I got ready to leave the house today. I found an ad in the Sunday paper for a temporary job. I needed a job badly. My finances were running out. I have not worked since January.

It has been 4 months now. I have been praying hard about it and I hoped this temporary position was still available.

I heated the water on the propane camp stove and filled my shower bag. I like to take my shower outside but this time I was in a hurry so I hung the bag up in the back room where I have fixed up a place to shower and wash my hair.

I put on my best skirt and blouse even tho it was a bit too hot for it today and started the mile and a half trek from the cabin to the car. The wind was up and by the time I got to the parking lot at the top of the trail I looked like a crazy woman. Long skirt, flushed face and hair standing out about a foot and a half on each side of my head. One of my neighbors was standing at the top of the trail when I came up with a big smile on his face. He seems to be a nice guy.

I said good morning and got in my car pulling my hair and my skirt in after me. When I looked in the mirror I realized why he had such a big smile on his face.

Good thing I keep a comb and brush and stuff like that in the car. I could not possibly interview for a job looking like the good witch of the woods. By the time I started using the spray, I had all the windows open and was not being bothered by a single black fly or mosquito!

I drove to Concord and after a bit of wrong turns finally found the place. I took the elevator to the 5th floor. Everyone seemed really friendly and smiled at me as we rode up. I smiled back.

I had faith that I was going to get this job. God knew I needed it. I had been telling Him for weeks. I found the office and went in. The receptionist was very friendly. Everyone smiled a lot. I knew this was the place for me.

I took the required tests. Math, grammar, typing and computer knowledge. I thanked God the math was adding long columns instead of algebra.

During the interview the woman was very friendly and seemed nice. She explained how this temp agency worked. Sometimes she looked down at her desk and when she looked up at me she had a gleam in her eye liked checked laughter about to burst forth. I could not imagine how much fun it would be to be working where everyone was so friendly.

I knew if it was the right job for me God would see to it and I did not have long to wait. They hired me on the spot and my first assignment will start next Monday.

I wanted to jump for joy as I tried gracefully to walk out of the office. It wasn't till I was walking toward the outside doors and caught a glimpse of myself in the glass that I realized why everyone was smiling. The elastic on my half slip had broken and my slip was hanging about 3 inches below my skirt! As I walked to the car, that slip started to slide and it fell to the ground just as I reached the car. I stepped out of it and picked it up and threw it on the car seat. Despite my fuzzy stiff hair and my misguided undergarment, my faith has proven true once again.

Getting that job was God. No one in their right mind would have hired someone who had very stiff hair that would not even move in the wind and a slip that was going south.

On the way home I began to laugh. Those people in that office must be having a field day with all this but I don't care, it really was very funny.

⸎

I not only got that job, but I went on to make a name for myself with the company. I worked temporary services for a long time. My boss never did forget that interview with the sliding slip and the stiff hair. I brought it up once after I had been with them awhile, and they all laughed out loud about it. The boss said she hired me on the spot because she thought if I could go through an interview with all that going on and never crack a smile then she knew I would be able to handle most of the employers they worked with.

Oswald Chambers in his book *Faith a Holy Walk* says, "Faith is not convincing ourselves that we have God's stamp of approval on our plans, it is believing that God's plans are better than ours. Biblical faith is not about taking risks, it's about taking on the identity of Jesus. It's not about having the audacity to do what is foolish, it is about having the courage to do what is difficult. It's not about running in the dark, it's about walking in the light. It's not about believing what people say about God, it's simply about believing what God says."

I had faith that day God would see me through and help me find the job I needed so I could continue to live out that time in my little wooded cabin. I knew I would still find the time to sit on rocks and write my stories. God always comes through for me. It is not sometimes what I want, but always what is best for me.

CHAPTER 11

Questions for God

I think God wants us to ask questions. I think He wants us to learn about Him and life on this earth. He wants us to learn in a way that gives us guidance and enhances our life here.

There certainly are a lot of questions:

Why are people so cruel to each other Lord?

Why do so many bad things happen?

Why, when we know the blessings of His presence, do we let the world's influence separate us from His love and His peace?

Why do we stray?

How do we know when we are not moving in the right direction?

How does my lack of faith hinder God's purpose for me?

How are my attempts to perfect myself keeping me from being and doing all that God wants for me?

How do I learn to love fully?

Oswald Chambers in *Faith A Holy Walk* asks the question, "Do I spend more energy pursuing what I want to achieve than I do in finding out what God wants me to believe?"

⟨✶✶⟩

Journal Entry

June 1997

Back at the Falls House. Larry is home and I am not house sitting for him now because he is home nights and weekends mostly. I have been house sitting for him in the winter since October 10ᵗʰ 1995. He was working as a long haul truck driver from October until about the end of June. He takes the summer off so I come here to live. When he is home on weekends, I usually come here then too. He was driving those really big propane and gas tanks all over the country this year. Last year, he was doing expediting or something like that all over the country. He only got home nine times last winter.

I started house sitting so I would not have to be here during the winter so much. I did a winter at this cabin and it is way too hard. I never got warm the whole winter. Walking was not an option it was more a necessity. In the winter I have to park my car a mile and a half away. I have nothing to prove to myself or anyone else for that matter.

Larry told me to stay at his place during the work week to avoid the two hour travel time and it does give me an opportunity to get to know him better. He has a fascinating sense of humor. I truly like the man. He has a very kind heart and tries not to show it. Kind of reminds me of my "adopted" Dad (Jess). He talks about God sometimes too. I truly believe God has put me here in NH and at Larry's house for a reason.

I seem to be getting to know God better too. I am finding it easier to get into His word now that I have set a routine. I have a lot of questions about life. His Word has the answers if we can just learn how to find them.

Now I study His Word because I want to. The Bible has some really good stories in it too and as a storyteller, I am more interested in studying them.

Then I will be reading one of them and find myself reading the next verses and chapters. Suddenly I have learned more than I planned and found the stories in different context and with clearer meanings!

Speaking of stories and storytelling, I have started new a guild called The Central New Hampshire Storytelling Guild. Started it last fall. We are planning our first Tellabration! It is an evening of storytelling for adults and kids who can sit and listen to stories for about an hour and a half. It is an international event that takes place all over the country on the same day. It is going to be in Franklin and in Milford at the same time so we are planning it with the help of the guilds. I am finding storytelling is a great outlet for my creativity. It is much more accepted as an art in New England then it is in Michigan. In Michigan I have been telling at some assisted living places and the museums and fairs and schools when my work allowed. Now here I will have to see what I can do. It is like starting a whole new career again but I think the possibilities are endless.

⚬⚬⚬

I have always felt loved in His presence, yet I have always had questions. I believe God wants us to question and learn in our hearts, not our heads.

One day when we are called home, we will know all the revelations of God. It is too big for us to know with our minds and in the context of this earth. Our questions are questions about this life and this presence on earth. We want to learn the how and why of things in the here and now. We are a curious bunch. We will find the answers to a lot of our questions by studying His Word

CHAPTER 12

Attitude of Gratitude

While I sat here thinking about writing today, it came to me that some of my thoughts show a lack of gratitude. I often catch myself complaining about this or that when it really is something I am glad to have.

I complain about the gas mileage of my car, but I love my car and it is essential to what I do. I complain about the commercials on TV, but I love the programs on the WORD channel and some of the HGTV or National Geographic programs. I complain about the weather if it is too cold, too hot or too rainy, but it is the rain that makes the plants grow.

I complain because the phone keeps ringing while I am trying to write, cook or do something else. However, without the phone I would have no business. I would not have access to friends or family or to emergency help.

The first year I had the Falls House, I didn't have a phone and cell phones were not for normal people. It was 1992. I remember having to walk up the hill about a half mile to get to my sister's house where there was a phone that worked (most of the time). The wire was strung through the woods from the main pole about a mile away. They had to run their own wire because they lived remotely, and the phone company would not come out without setting poles and charging mega bucks. They ran the wire up in the trees and along the road to their house. It often would get wet in the splices or animals would break it. The best thing was it worked most of the time.

Journal entry

September 1997

At the Falls House for the weekend. The half log stairs to the sleeping loft have tilted even more over the year. They are worn smooth with use. When I am not careful I slide right down on my behind. Especially easy to do when I have sox on my feet. I did that in the middle of the night when I was up to go to the bathroom. I bet I have bruises.

I woke early this morning and pulled my feet out of the covers and set up on the side of the bed. It is part of my morning ritual to have my clothes ready to put on beside the bed and to check the sky for signs of the day. As I reached for my pants, I looked out across the room to the windows that faced East. I am not sure how I managed it but within seconds I had my pants on my shoes in my hands and was down the stairs without falling or hitting my head on the beam. I ran outside. What was I going to do? I could not see the fire from the back yard. I ran around to the front. I could not see it from the front either but I caught a faint hint of wood smoke.

Fire in the woods where no fire truck could get would spell disaster not only for me and the Falls House but also for many animals and the people who also had homes or camps deep in the woods around me. What was I to do? My mind was racing but my body did not know what to do next.

I would have to run up to my sisters and use her phone to call the fire department but first I needed to see where the fire was so I could give them an accurate description of the location.

I still could not see the fire from on the ground so I went back in the house and looking out the windows didn't help either. I guess the only way to spot it was up in the loft. It wasn't till I set back down on the edge of the bed that I saw it. A trail of raising fog that had touched the top of those fire colored trees looked like smoke. I began to laugh. Whew, it was a good thing I had not called the fire department. I was embarrassed just thinking of it.

I went down stairs and lit the small fire in the wood cook stove and started the coffee. I was grateful for the day and for not having a fire in the woods. I was grateful that I did not have to run up through the woods to call a fire department that would not be able to do much except try to contain it. I was grateful no one saw me acting like a Henny Penny running around yelling "the sky is falling, the sky is falling." I was grateful for the place and the peace that surrounded me as I drank my first cup. I was grateful that I could laugh at myself and my jump to conclusions and that none of my fear was founded in reality.

It strikes me that one of the first things we teach our kids when they learn to speak is to say please and thank you. We want them to show their gratitude. If it is so important to us to have our kids be thankful, how much more important might it be to show our gratitude to a Father who has given so much?

David continually thanks the Father in the Psalms. The words "give thanks" appear twenty-four times. The Israelites had thank offerings at their feasts. This is not a new concept.

"Oh give thanks unto the Lord for He is good. His mercy endures forever" appears in both the first and the last verses of Psalm 118. NAS. If He says it twice in the same passage, it must be very important. This is both a request and a promise. The request "Give thanks to the Lord" and the promise "His mercy endures forever."

Today was one of those days when just a couple of words set me off. It was hard to get back an attitude of gratitude.

I did not want to go to church so I started sewing. The hurt stayed with me and my mind was doing its thing. "Why do people say things that hurt my feelings? What's wrong with me now? No one understands me. They are all so selfish and self-centered. Blah, blah, blah…" I knew I needed an attitude adjustment. I decided I better go to church because I sure wasn't going to get it here. I put the roast in the crock pot and went to church. I am glad I did.

The pastor gave a really good sermon today. He acted out the part of a news caster at WBZX in Boston during February 1944. He was telling about the sinking of a ship and how many people were saved by the four chaplains on board. They calmed the panicked men down, created order and put them in lifeboats. One chaplain was Jewish priest, one was a Catholic priest, two were Protestant preachers. They handed out life jackets and put men in the few life boats that were left until there were no more life jackets to give out. Then with one accord they gave their life jackets to four sailors, kneeled together and prayed as they sank with the ship.

I know there are many people who have it a lot worse than I do. I know I was not being thankful for what God had given me. I knew I had to praise God and give those feelings I was having to God. I knew if I did nothing about this feeling, I would end up being resentful.

I came home in a better mood, felt grateful for the things I have, the place where I live, and God's unending love and grace.

I need to keep my attitude of gratitude and thanksgiving. God has put me here for a reason. I know that. I have much to do to make this place a better environment. I pray that God will give me a song in my heart and a smile on my face tomorrow when I wake. I do not want to let my feet hit the floor before I say, "Thank you God for another beautiful, bountiful day."

I am so blessed to be able to do what God wants me to do, and to be able to go to church, read a book, or cook a roast in the crock pot. I am blessed and I am grateful.

Yesterday it rained most of the day. At one time there was a rainbow. It was my sign that God would be there for me. I didn't need a sign but when I saw it I held onto it and I am glad I did. It reminded me that things would get better, and that all things work together for good for those who love the Lord.

We want our children to be grateful for what they have and what they are given. We want them to show their gratitude. How much more do we need to show God our own gratefulness?

CHAPTER 13

Worship

Psalm 96: 1-4

"O sing to the Lord a new song; sing to the Lord all the earth! Sing to the Lord, bless His name; show forth His salvation from day to day. Declare His Glory among the nations, His marvelous works among all the peoples. For great is the Lord and greatly to be praised; He is to be reverently feared and worshiped above all." (NIV)

When I was a young adult, church and worship seemed synonymous. Then as a young mother I decided going to church was important to the way I wanted to raise my child. After she became an adult I did "church" mostly by myself. I had decided I didn't need a church building or its people to worship God. I usually worshiped outside in the woods. One of the reasons I bought the Falls House was so I could spend time by myself with God, and part of that time was spent in worship.

I quit going to church because my "church friends" turned their backs on me just when I needed them most. I did not need hypocritical people with their "holier than thou" attitudes talking behind my back and then giving me a hug when they saw me.

Life got real busy, and I didn't bother about church or worship for a while. Then I decided I wanted a closer walk with God. You can't really have a closer walk without worship.

I started caretaking some property for a friend that was out of state for a while. It was a very peaceful spot. I would go out and just sit in the woods or down by the lake. Sometimes I would sit right out in the open field in the sun. I would get quiet and thank God for all those beautiful places to just be. I would pray and worship Him with songs. What did it matter? No one could hear me except God, and He loves me just the way I am. He doesn't care if I can't carry a tune in a bucket.

When I came to New Hampshire, the Falls House offered the same kind of peace and ability to worship God. Maybe even more so, because it was mine and I could be there every day.

⬳⬲⬳

Journal Entry

Summer 2009

Usually I do outdoor church at the Falls House but today I did outdoor church at home. I walked the woods and the pasture. I sat on a rock outcropping overlooking the valley. The dogs and the cats all had to come with me. It is strange walking cats. They run ahead and try to anticipate where we are going. The dogs just love to go whatever direction I point them in. The cats will discover they got it wrong and catch up and rub on the dogs like they have just found their mommy. I have to laugh at them.

I have been checking out the churches in the area off and on since I came here in 1995. I haven't really found one I liked till now. I went to a lot of different ones. Some I visited more than once and one time I actually went to the same one for a year or so whenever I was in town. But it just wasn't what I wanted. Wasn't quite a good fit. I know I can worship God whenever and wherever I want to but sometimes I just want to be with people who believe the way I do and really want to worship Him.

Am I being judgmental? Yes I am. At first it was just because I knew I could not depend on people. But as I began to walk closer to God it was more discerning than judgmental. I want to worship where I feel welcome and where people will accept me for who I am and where I can do the same. I want to worship where people are not afraid to talk about God and His minions. I want to know that we will all pray for each other.

Finally I found a little church like that where the people are friendly. I have grown so much that I don't really worry much about what they think and I have learned my lesson about putting my faith in people instead of God. I don't have to be anything or anyone that God has not called me to be. I keep reminding myself "it's not my do but my who that counts."

It is important for me to keep understanding that people are just people and no one is perfect. If we were we would not need God. It is the Holy Spirit who is my guide. As long as I go to worship Him and put Him first above all others, I will not get hurt by the attitude of other people.

I am committed to Christ and to listening to God and being blessed by the presence of the Holy Spirit. My God is an awesome God. His grace is all I need.

I have been praying about this church and becoming a member. It means commitment. Am I ready for that?

Journal Entry

December 2012

I did decide to join the church and to sit back and see what that means and where God was leading me. I have a tendency to jump right into things with both feet and do whatever I see needs to be done. It seems God has put me on a shelf for a while. Whenever I decide to help on some project or try to do something in this church God pulls me back. He seems to be telling me that I don't need to do that. God seems to be using others in this church and telling me He doesn't need me to be "doing" things.

He knows I get really passionate about the things I do. I find it easy to take over and just do things. He has other people in mind for these jobs at this church.

I know that whenever one door closes another one opens but sometimes it takes a while before it begins to swing wide. Sometimes there is a resting time.

I guess it is time to become a sponge and soak in all the love and joy and knowledge of God I can. Time now to lean on Him and make space in my life for the next big thing. Seed – Time- Harvest. Guess I am in the Time part.

Learning to hold back and let God use others to do His will has been a challenge. I often have "helium hand" when people ask for volunteers. My hand just shoots up of its own volition. I have to sit on it or before I know it, I have so many projects and things to do I begin to get stressed about getting them all done.

I have learned to wait and be still and know when it is God calling.

I have found a place to worship Him where I feel welcome and at home, where I can do small things that make a difference, where people seem to believe the way I do and try to live out their lives the way Christ would want them to.

I have learned to worship Him in many ways and many places:

I worship Him by singing in the car on the way to somewhere.

I worship Him with thanksgiving.

I worship Him with my tithe.

I worship Him by listening to His voice.

I worship Him by being obedient.

I worship Him with joy and laughter.

I worship Him by helping others.

There are many ways of worshiping God.

How do you worship?

CHAPTER 14

It's All About His Grace

His power reveals itself in my weakness. There is nothing I can do but that does not need God's power and grace to give it life.

In *America the Beautiful* there is a line that says, "America, America God shed His grace on thee and crown thy good with brotherhood from sea to shining sea."

What is God's grace? I checked both the *Strong's Bible Dictionary* and *Webster's Dictionary*. *Webster's Dictionary* defined grace as "divine love and protection given to mankind from God. Also good will and favor." *Strong's Bible Dictionary* explains it as: "good will, gratitude, benefit given as well as all the beauty and gracefulness of movement and other pleasing qualities."

Many preachers and evangelists are now preaching the message of grace. Their sermons have gone from reinforcing the philosophy of work equals reward in God's kingdom to the truth of God's will for us to receive His grace.

Reflecting on the secrets of His grace brings me to realize that it isn't what you do that is important. You can't earn your salvation, nor can you gain status in God's kingdom by what you do. It isn't about your do, it is about your who. Who you are in Christ is what brings to you the ability to accept God's gifts of grace.

God cannot give you grace and favor unless you accept it. I picture a Father with his hand and arm outstretched. In His hand is a gift. We are not sure what that gift is. We do not know what the trick is, or whether there is a cost for accepting this gift so we hesitate. We hem and haw for a bit and scuff our feet. We want that gift badly, but what about the monsters lurking to jump and grab you? Is this a trap? Does this gift come with strings attached?

God the Father will not force us to take His gift of grace. He will wait until we walk up and put our hand out. He will wait until we are ready to receive it. He also will not give us more than we can handle.

Like the Israelites getting manna, God gave them what they needed and told them not to horde or save any over. When they took what they did not need, it went sour. God will give us the grace we need and can handle. He will give us the grace to go through the wilderness, and when we have achieved the Promised Land, He will only give us as much as we can handle.

We have the responsibility to accept the grace that is so freely given with gratitude.

❦❦

Journal Entry

January 2013

Michelle and I were in a hurry to pick up printing and supplies on our way to a meeting today. She does not really believe in God's favor. It was her opinion that she did not deserve God's grace and favor, therefore she could not receive it.

I sometimes forget I am talking out loud and I said "Okay Lord. We really need to make it to this meeting on time. Please give us the grace and favor we need to get this done." She laughed but just as we came to the front of the store a parking place opened up and I pulled right into it. Not more than a few feet from the entrance.

Then I said "Thank you so much Father for giving us your grace. Please let it be with us throughout this day." She didn't laugh when the printing was ready and waiting for us. Nor when there was enough money on a gift card to pay for it. She was quiet when we got a front row parking place at the event and again when we got all the things that we needed to carry this workshop through to the end.

On the way home she said to me "That is all good. You probably deserve God's grace for all you do!" I explained to her that it isn't my do but my who. I am a child of God adopted into His family. Heir to the throne with Jesus. It wouldn't be able to happen if I was not willing to accept the grace of God. Like a gift that someone gives you, if you do not take it out of their hand and open it up and accept it with gratitude, they cannot give it to you. So it is with God's grace and favor. He can hold it in his outstretched hand but if you are not willing to reach out with you words, thoughts and gratitude, He cannot force you to take it.

I didn't always believe in God's grace and favor either. It has taken me years to get over the fact that I know I do not deserve any kind of favors. If I had to depend on what I do and how "good" I am, I would probably starve to death or be homeless.

Faith comes into it too. As I learn to walk closer with God, my faith becomes stronger and I know that God's Grace is all I need.

⌒⌘⌒

Where fear abounds, faith falls down. Fear is the opposite of faith. An acronym of Fear is False Evidence Appearing Real. If you are fearful of the gifts God gives to you and the grace and favor He showers on you, you will not be able to receive them. You will miss out on much of what God has to offer, all because you do not feel that you are worthy. Don't forget, you don't deserve anything God gives to you. You did not earn your salvation, and you cannot ever be worthy of His love.

You can know that you are a child of God, adopted into His family. As His child, God the Father will shower onto you all the Grace and favor you can stand. God is happy to extend His gifts to you the same way you want to give good things to your children or grandchildren. Do they say, "No thanks, I am not worthy of these gifts"? Of course they don't. They squeal with delight. Learn to accept the love and grace of God with gladness and gratitude.

Ask God for His grace every morning before you start your day. Notice the way God opens doors or closes ones that are no longer meant for your good. Keep notes in your journal of the grace and favor of God in your life.

CHAPTER 15

His Timing is Perfect

I seem to always be in a hurry these days, always managing two or three things at once. Funny, I don't remember taking juggling lessons but somehow that is what it feels like. Timing is everything. It is funny how that works. My timing is nothing like God's timing.

Sometimes I think the new lie of the enemy is being busy makes us important. We eat a breakfast sandwich on the way to somewhere. We drive off with our morning coffee in our hand. We don't take time to reflect on what we want the day to bring before we are out the door. It is as though every minute of every day has to be filled with some activity, or something is wrong. We even set the alarm on our cell phones to beep us into action when we should be on our way to the next best thing.

Journal entry

September 1998

I was late calling "Mom" today. We call each other alternating Sundays usually about 2pm and I had storytelling to do this afternoon so it was 5 before I got a chance to call. She wasn't feeling good today. It is hard to talk to her when she doesn't feel well so I mostly listened.

She kept asking me what I wanted of her things. I told her the only thing I really wanted was for her to get better. She said "you don't understand Lauretta, I am not getting well, I am dying." I said "I know mom, but that doesn't mean I want you too. If I had my druthers you would stay around for a very long time." I could hear the smile in her voice. She said "I wish so too but my wishing and your wishing isn't going to make it happen. It is up to God and His timing. When it is my time to go, I will be gone."

She will be happy to be with the Lord I know but I sure won't be happy without her. I have experienced loss many times and this one is going to be tough. I know it will be sooner than I want and a lot sooner than I expect. God's timing isn't always ours.

I finally told her I would take the ruby colored glass dishes that were hers and her mothers. I already have a few pieces that were my birth mom's and her mothers. I figure she won't know where they are or be able to get to them for a while so I won't need to worry about a place to put them right away.

Journal Entry

August 1999

Sunday afternoons are hard for me still. Mom died in April and I still go to pick up the phone and call her about 2 o'clock and then I remember. Sometimes during the week, I still think of something I want to talk over with her and catch myself reaching for the phone. I have even dialed the number before I thought of it. Old habits and old loves are hard to let go of.

She gave me the red dishes at Christmas. She had them sitting in the living room in a box when I got there. I use them for lunch and smile as I see them. I am not sure how she got to them but she did it. Determined was a word many people would use to describe her. Stubborn? This apple didn't fall too far from that tree I guess.

I miss her so much. I probably always will. I still miss my first mom and she died when I was just about ready to turn 16. I miss my grandpa and he died when I was 6. My memories of them are still fresh in some ways. I can recall so many things they both did and said and those recollections make me smile. I know I was not an easy child. I know this loss will be a sweet memory for me too in time. I just have to get to that place in my heart first. More growing to do.

Journal Entry

September 2010

I have been crying out to God for help again. It is so hard being so far away and having my daughter sick. I chose to live here but I didn't plan on things being so hard sometimes. The timing is all wrong and it is almost impossible for me to get off work for an extended length of time right now.

I just want her to get well. I pray for her every day. I can hear mom say "God answers prayer in His own way and in His own time." His time isn't necessarily when I want things done. He says you have not because you ask not so I ask. But I don't want to wait. I want it now.

Funny how that happens isn't it. I wait to ask until it becomes crucial and then I want the answer right now. Oh dear!

God's timing is different than ours that is for sure. Ecclesiastes 3:1 says

"To everything there is a season and a time for everything under heaven." (NAS)

I don't think heaven goes by daylight savings time.

I don't think it was God's intention that we always be so busy that we cannot enjoy the fruit of our labor.

Ecclesiastes 3: 12-13

> I know that there is nothing better for them to be glad and get and do good as long as they live ... and also that every man should eat and drink and enjoy the good of all his labor it is the gift of God. (NAS)

John 10:10

> The thief comes only to steal and destroy but I came so you might have and enjoy life and have it in abundance to the full till it overflows. (NAS)

When we are too busy, we forget the time that we set aside to spend with the Father. We often say "I will do it later." But later never comes. It is the plan of the enemy to keep us so busy that we do not have time for each other. We don't have time to demonstrate our love for one another, and we don't have time to sit still and listen to the still small voice that is God.

But what about God's timing? It is definitely different than ours. He knows what He has planned for us. His timing is perfect, and we often don't even know it.

It is sometimes so hard to wait for God's answer. I ask Him to take care of something, and then I try to figure out on my own what to do to fix the situation. I often wait to give things to God until the situation becomes critical, and then I say, "Here God, fix this, but please do it now".

Time is mentioned in 765 Bible verses. One of the scriptures that reaches out to me is about seed, time and harvest. Planting the seed and letting it wait for a time to open up, grow and bear its fruit. A lot of the growth depends on the time it takes. If you pick something like a tomato too soon, it does not have the flavor of one that you let ripen on the vine. It needs that time in the sunshine to develop the flavor and richness that makes it special. It is the same with us. We need the time with our Father and His Son to develop our richness of spirit and the maturity that lets God take over. The knowledge that gives us the wisdom to say what we need to, or keep our mouth shut when we don't need to comes with that maturity. The wisdom to know what others need from us comes from that time of waiting. The gifts God has given us to use for His glory need time to develop and time to find where He wants us to use them.

One of the fruits of the spirit is patience. Patience becomes a part of us as we grow closer in our walk with God. We need to have patience to let God take on these challenges and make things right, patience to know that God will make everything right in His time, patience to accept that although we think God is late in coming, that His timing is perfect.

There is a song titled *When He's Four Days Late* that has a line in the chorus that asks this question: "Isn't it great that when He's four days late, He's still on time?" The song is the story of Lazarus. John 11 tells us about the illness and death of Lazarus, and how Mary and Martha sent for Jesus knowing that if He came He could save their brother.

When Jesus heard the message He said, "This sickness is not to end in death, but for the glory of God, so that the Son of God may be glorified by it." (NAS)

When Jesus heard that Lazarus was sick He stayed where He was two days longer! Then He went to Judea where Lazarus and his sisters Mary and Martha lived. The story tells us that when Jesus asked to have the stone covering rolled away from Lazarus' tomb, Martha said "Lord by this time there will be a stench because he has been dead for four days." Jesus was four days late, yet it was perfect timing to show the glory of God and His Son. Jesus called Lazarus forth from the grave for the glory of God. Many of the Jews who came to the grave with Mary and Martha believed in Him because of this.

God's timing is perfect every time.

CHAPTER 16

Healing

I was twenty-one when I had my first bout with cancer. The C word. I was terrified. My mother had passed away when I was fifteen with the big C word. I knew that I was going to go the way of my mother and leave a ten month old baby behind. Back in those days treatments weren't gentle and surgery was the first and often the only option. After a hysterectomy and a nineteen day stay in the hospital, the doctor said he "thought" they got it all. Well if he thought that was reassuring, he was wrong! I worried about it for months. I was already too thin, and I just kept losing weight. Finally life got in the way. I had too many other things to worry about. I worried about finding a way to get an education so I could provide for my baby girl, and keeping up with a husband who liked to surprise me with a move every few months.

I worked in the healthcare field. I saw the miracles of healing that happened and I saw some that didn't happen. It reaffirmed my faith for others, but not particularly for me. Well after all, I did not deserve any grace from God. That was for sure. Look how far I had strayed. Look at all I had done wrong. Look at all I had not done.

A car accident that caused me to be unable to walk for a few months and a couple of critical illnesses brought me closer to understanding God's healing power, but still I felt was not worthy.

Thirty-five years after the first cancer, I was diagnosed with breast cancer. Oh boy, what could I do? What should I do? Where could I go to get the best information so I could make a good decision? What if it was fatal?

This time there was a difference. I had started to grow up. It had taken me an unusually long time, but I was not a baby Christian anymore. I had started on the journey to find a closer walk with God. I knew God would clear the path of the debris left from my sin cluttered life that had been my path before. I knew He would open the door for healing and growth. I had stopped living in the fear of the moment and was living in faith with the Father. By this time I knew I did not need to be worthy of healing. As a matter of fact, I knew I would never be worthy of God's healing or His love. We can never be worthy. How could flawed us be worthy of a love so deep that He could and would give His only begotten Son so that He could bring us into God's presence? We can't be worthy of that kind of love but we don't have to be. God does not want us to be perfect. He sees us through Jesus who is perfect for us. Just the fact that He loves us is good enough.

The following journal entries are not all of the entries in this special journal. They are the ones that seem to fit here and that I feel comfortable sharing.

Cancer Journal Entry

May 1998

I have decided to write about this cancer journey in a special healing journal. Not along with the daily chatter or occurrences. It needs its own space.

Everything seemed to move real fast after I got the message that my mammogram showed a spot in the right breast. The radiologist called and had me set up an appointment with the local surgeon right away. Funny that the radiologist called and not my regular doctor. First a visit with the surgeon, then a lumpectomy and another visit with the surgeon and not a word from my doctor. The surgeon says it is cancer and I need to start radiation and chemotherapy right away. I said no. I want a second opinion. I feel in my heart that all of this is not necessary.

Cancer Journal Entry

June 1998

Got the 2nd opinion. This Dr said I did not need to do anything. That it looks as though they got it all and I don't need to worry about it anymore. Just have regular checkups. I don't know who to believe. They are two extremes on opposite ends.

Cancer Journal Entry

November 1998

My new doctor referred me to Darthmouth Cancer Center. They have a whole team that works with you. I had some new tests and another lumpectomy. Excising the area around the original sight. Seems they wanted to make sure first surgeon did get it all. Glad I came to Dartmouth. The team here explains all the options and makes suggestions. You get to make the decisions on your own health care. They say I don't really need to do any radiation or chemo right now. They want to keep checking on it tho just in case and I think that is a great idea. Cancer is scary even tho I know my God is there right with me and right with the doctor and nurses.

They suggested and I concur that I don't need to do anything at the present except keep an eye on it.

I have to admit my emotions have been all over the place. I have had a tough time with it. I keep having to give it back to God. I keep taking it back and worrying. Sheesh.

Cancer Journal Entry

January 1999

Checkups every 3 months seem to be going very well. It is always stressful though. Go have a mammogram and see the doctor and then wait to make sure the results of the mammogram are ok. There always seems to be a lot of waiting involved. I am getting better at waiting I think.

Cancer Journal Entry

December 1999

Finally down to once a year with the checkups. Funny, I barely think of it unless I get one of those pains that tell me the scar tissue is still there or something. Doctor said 5 years was the date. If you make it through 5 years all clear you probably have it beat.

Cancer Journal Entry

May 2000

Shoot 2 days after my 2 year mammogram I got the call. Happy Birthday to me! On my birthday no less. The doctor from Dartmouth called. They want me back up there for more tests. Saw another spot. I have to admit I cried. I almost sat down and had a real pity party. Almost is the key word. I just know it is all going to be okay so why waste a good party?

Needle biopsy was excruciatingly painful. Not supposed to be I guess. They just could not hit the spot as it was too far back so they stuck some needles in there before we went into surgery so the doctor could tell where he was supposed to look. I knew it would all be okay after we prayed with the surgeon before they took me in.

Back to regular checkups and mammograms.

Cancer Journal Entry

September 2000

Okay so this time it appears to be more serious. It's back. I was really down at first. I just wanted to crawl up on my Father's lap and stay there for a long while. But when fear showed up and I found myself getting ready to have a big pity party, I changed courses. When things get tough the tough get going. I spend a lot of time singing in the car. Praising God gives me hope and lifts my spirits.

Cancer Journal Entry

January 2001

More surgery. They are taking this poor breast off piece by piece. Sheesh!!

Scheduled radiation treatments for early in the morning so I can drive up to Dartmouth in the morning and get back in time for work. 36 treatments.

There is a lady here who has the same kind of cancer I have. She is really having a pity party. Been having one a long time I think. The radiation is making her sick. She is high strung and cross and I can only help by making her smile once in a while. She is pretty sick. I told her I would pray for her and she said yes please do. The thought seemed to help her relax a little.

I don't seem to be getting sick from the radiation. I am tired but I am taking some protein shakes to keep up my energy level so I can actually work. I have a ton of stuff to do at work and can't really afford to take time off right now. The extra protein and the slowed metabolism are making me gain weight.

What is the difference between her cancer and mine? Not much. We both had the same amount. We both had surgery. We both are having 36 radiation treatments. Her radiation is probably as strong as mine. The difference is in the attitude. Knowing God is in this is helpful and it also gives me strength and joy.

I have to admit I am pretty tired when I get home from work at night. I have the treatments and then go to work and work all day. Then it is home to fix supper. I am sometimes just too tired to want to eat.

Cancer Journal Entry

February 1, 2001

Today is Lesa's birthday and Dad is passing away. This is a really tough day for both her and I. I needed to do the last 5 treatments the day I got on a plane to fly to Michigan to be with him. Seems if we didn't do those treatments we would have to start over or something wouldn't be right or something like that. I don't know but we did them three in the morning and two more in the afternoon. Sometimes you just have to do what ya gotta do. So glad my God is with me on this journey. I couldn't do it alone. Those last treatments were tough. Burned a bit but it turned out ok. Hey maybe I will glow in the dark.

Cancer Journal Entry

February 2, 2001

Got to be with dad when he passed and He was glad we were there. He has been in assisted living for a long time. Mom passed away 2 years ago and Dad still missed her and sometimes when he was functioning he talked about her. He really started going downhill at Christmas. Sitting around and not being able to take care of himself has never been his style. We were all here and we held hands and prayed with him. I have been so blessed to have two dads and two moms. Barb and Jess were my second family after my birth mom passed away. I miss both of them a lot. Lesa has had a special connection with both Barb and Jess and she is going to miss them as much as I do. She was worried about me having all those treatments but she knew I would be there for her and Dad.

Now it is back to check ups and mammograms.

Cancer Journal Entry

May 2005

Five years and all clear. That was the magic number according to the statistics.

This one hit me real hard. 5 years all clear again and now it is on the other side. Different type this time. Much more aggressive and rapid growing tumor. One small one to start out with and within 2 weeks it was bigger and had 5 other suspicious areas in there with it.

Choices to make. Chemotherapy and radiation or surgery chemo and radiation or mastectomy? Prayed real had about it. I think a mastectomy is the way to go. I am not happy about it at all. It is different this time but I am at peace with the decision. There are really caring people at Dartmouth. They explain everything fully and show they care. That sure makes a big difference.

This whole thing has thrown my emotions into a whirlwind. I feel like crying and often just want to be alone. I try not to worry or show how upset I am. I go to work and do my job and if I am quiet and a little distracted most people just think I am really busy. It is true. I really am busy right now. I just don't have time to deal with this.

Larry is just steady through it all. He is caring and understanding. What a gift.

Cancer Journal Entry

June 2005

The surgery went well and I have to have this drain thing for a while. The doctor seemed pleased that we pray with him before we go into surgery. I know it helps me to relax. My God is awesome. I know in my heart that He has been here with me through this whole thing. He has held me when I wanted to cry and stood me on my feet when I needed to be strong. He didn't just heal me in a flash of lightening or anything like that but His being there made it all much easier. I am here because He isn't through with me yet. Still under construction I think.

Cancer Journal Entry

September 2005

Back to three month checkups. Then it goes to six months and then back to yearly.

Ten years have passed. I am still doing mammograms and waiting for the answers once a year and I am still getting the all clear. I can't say it has been a walk in the park. It has been very challenging in many ways. I have had to have a couple of biopsies, but God's healing hand has been on me all the way. Without Him I would not have healed so fast or so well after the mastectomy. I did not even take one of the prescribed pain pills. I just didn't need them. My God is an awesome God. I can't say that part of this journey has been without emotional bumps, but I can say He was there all the time. It is hard to believe that it has been ten years already. When I think of it, it doesn't seem so long ago.

Each time I go for a checkup my first thoughts are "What if I have it again? What if it is worse? What if?" There is always a few minutes that I begin to do the "what ifs". I realize this is fear not faith that is talking. God did not say we wouldn't feel fear, but He did say He would be with us and we shouldn't act in fear.

Soon the "what ifs" turn into "so whats". So what if it does come back? So what if the next time I have a checkup there are some questions? SO WHAT? God will take care of me. He will see me through. He might not heal me with a flash of lightening and smoke. He might not call someone to lay hands on me and heal me. He might not heal me at all. But so what? God will see me through and bring me home in His own time. We never know the time, but for right now I will go on working and praying, learning and growing. I am still under construction. God isn't through with me yet.

CHAPTER 17

A Circular Journey

Life is a circular journey from birth to death to life. God is the inventor, the author of life. He is all powerful and all love. It is only from His breath and His Word that we have life at all.

This life of mine has taken some very strange twists and turns, and yet all the time I have known that God was there with me. When I strayed too far off the path He was waiting for me to return to the spot I derailed. He never condemned me, but welcomed me home with open arms. I learned I could call Him Father and crawl upon His lap for comfort when I needed to.

⌘

Journal Entry

January 2015

Still no New Year's resolutions but still the list of goals. I am still on the journey to get to know God better.

It is strange how life has a way of bringing you back around to the place you stepped off the trail. It comes full circle.

This journey that I am on began with that first scream as I entered this world. Mom was tired out from the carrying and giving birth to a baby just 18 months after the first one. Dad was disappointed because he wanted a boy. Both were glad that I had such a healthy set of lungs.

At 6 or 7 months old I learned I could get picked up and held by my father if I piled all the blankets and pillows and stuff in the corner of the crib and climbed up and fell out. I did it over and over. Already I craved being held by the Father. Was it a trace of a memory of our Heavenly Father that caused me to crave this attention? I don't know. Does a spirit remember whence it came? Was it that empty spot inside of me that longs for the presence of God?

From a shy little girl who hid behind her mother and followed her dad around to an adolescence of abuse and betrayal. From a young woman who married to escape a life in which she felt alone and abandoned to a young mother who knows she has only herself and sometimes God to rely on. From mother to grandmother sometimes struggling sometimes not, sometimes following the path God had set out for me and often times straying far off that good road, led astray by the desire to be loved. Always searching for that Father that would never betray. Searching for that love that would not condemn or seek to destroy or control.

Searching. Always searching until I finally came to the end of myself at the place where there was only God.

It is hard to describe someone who has always known and believed in God who could still need to come to the end of themselves in such a way. But I did. I needed to get to the place where all there was left was God in order for me to let Him take my hand and lead me where He wanted me to be.

I often came to Him when I was in need or lonely or in trouble of some kind but when things were going well, I pretty much led my own life. I did my own thing. I guess I thought I had to do it my way. I could not trust anyone and I really was not sure I could trust God. So one day after yet another failed relationship and another night or maybe a week of drinking and weeping in one of the biggest pity parties I had ever thrown myself, God said to me through a voice on the radio "You can be pitiful or you can be powerful but you can't be both pitiful and powerful"

Any other time I would have stood up and said "YES, I CAN DO THIS MYSELF. I DON'T NEED ANYONE ELSE." Not this time tho. Sitting on the floor alone beside the open window in that apartment over that garage in 1989, I knew in my heart of hearts that the only way to get through this and not have to keep doing it over and over was to get it right.

Suddenly I knew that my heavenly Father was waiting for me to crawl up on His lap and rest. It was time for me to let Him lead and He did.

He took the worst of my messes and made them Master pieces. He showed me that the way to be loved was to accept His all-encompassing love and to open up and share that love in whatever way He provided for me.

It has been a long and fruitful journey. If I had it to do over, would I? Yes but maybe I would not have made so many mistakes along the way. Or maybe I would. Without all those times of trial and times of joy, would I be the same person I am today? Would I be so in love with God? Would I be able to help people the same way? Maybe, maybe not. Only God can answer those questions.

It is funny how sometimes you can see better looking back than looking forward. Looking back on this journey I can see its twists and turns. It has bends I did not see around. It has distractions and disasters that were waiting for me to stumble into.

It has been difficult and I have had to walk through many fairly disastrous situations but I know I have always had God with me from that first cry at birth and I will have until I am in that place that has all the answers to my questions.

But now it is different. Now instead of yelling help me Lord I am more often than not asking "How can I help Lord? What can I do?" How can I show your love?"

New years list of goals

Get to know God better and walk closer with Him.

Find a way each day to bless someone else.

Finish the book.

Work on telling and teaching storytelling.

Put together workshops for Christian Storytelling Conference in June.

There were many more things on that New Year's list of goals that would just take up space and not add to this book, so we will let go of them here and let God take care of them.

I got a story in the email the other day from a friend who got it from a friend who did not know where they got it. I think it has been passed along a lot and is what we would call an urban legend. I would like to share it with you.

The five year old boy and his parents were at the veterinarian's. They had brought the old dog in. He was sick and not going to live long. Everyone was feeling sad about the loss of this beloved pet. The father said to the vet, "I just don't know why our dogs can't live as long as we do." The boy spoke up, "I know." The three adults turned to him. The boy said, "We are here to learn to love. Dogs already know how to do that so they don't have to stay so long."

Wise words from a very young child. We are here to learn to love and be loved. We were created to love God.

I think God wants us to ask questions and to look beyond ourselves to find the answers we crave.

In the meantime, I am still holding on to His hand for dear life. And a dear life it is. So the journey continues. It comes full circle. I hope some of the lessons I have learned will help you on your walk with the Father. I know that each of us has to travel our own path. I know that the Father is there walking beside each of us. He is there to pick us up when we don't think we can go on, and He is there smiling as we laugh at our silliness and our hearts fill with joy and happiness. He is shared in stories and in our love for each other. He is in the sunset and the sunrise. Spend some time with Him. Let Him help you grow.

Stepping into the Light

Just when I thought this book was complete I realized from a conversation with a friend that there was one thing left to do. My friend said they had been thinking a lot about faith lately, not spirituality but faith. They were interested in learning more about faith and was going to read my book as soon as it came out.

Where does faith come from? It comes from knowing deep down inside the center of your being that there is a God. Knowing that God is for you. If God is for you who can be against you?

When you come to the place where you know inside that God exists, but you still have are so many doubts and questions, get on your knees. You don't have to have fancy words, you just have to open your heart. Pray for guidance, strength and knowledge. Pray for Him to come into your heart and show you the way.

It's not about the trappings and rituals of religion. It is about relationship. Realize you are a part of the family of God. You are an adopted child. Know who you are in Christ.

Leave all your baggage at the cross. You don't have to carry those burdens anymore. You are free. Every time you are tempted to go back and pick one of them up, remember how heavy it actually is. You are light and free. Don't weigh yourself down like Marley's ghost in the story *A Christmas Carole*. Guilt and shame have no part in you anymore. Anger and hatred only act like salt on the root of a plant. It kills the vine. Remember John 10:10 "The thief comes only to steal, kill and destroy, I come that you might have and enjoy your life abundantly and to the full." (AV)

Hebrews 11:1 "Faith is the substance of things hoped for, the evidence of things not seen"(KJ) The place in your spirit that has been an empty dark hole, will suddenly be empty no more. It will be filled with a knowing you won't be able to describe, and you will feel finally at home. Tears may flow and they will be tears of relief and joy. It isn't that you won't question or doubt, it is that you will know deep in your soul that God is, even when you have those questions.

Faith is a tiny seed. Who does understand the death of a tiny seed when it breaks apart and lies in the dark fragrant earth waiting? The seed is waiting for the nourishment from the earth, the cleansing hydration of cooling rain and the comforting warmth of the sun. It is waiting for the sun to reach deep inside and find the sprout that pushes its way heavenward, reaching for the light. Don't choke it off with fear. Fear is the opposite of faith and does not come from God. Feed it with His Word. Water it with His love. Give it light and watch it flourish and grow. It will hold you in good stead when you are in need.

Faith is the line that was always being disconnected becoming repaired permanently, giving us open lines of communication. It is the relief of knowing you don't have to hide anything because He already knows and He loves you anyway.

Being filled with faith is being so filled with excitement and joy that you want to tell someone about it. You want to shout it from the roof top.

Faith is the quiet place you sit and breathe and know deep inside that God is with you.

When the newness wears off and joy fades a little, you have questions and need to know more. It is the baby learning to walk and sometimes falling down. You will get off the path sometimes too, but you will always know He is there for you whenever you need Him.

Take it one step at a time. You may not learn things the way I did. Each of us learns in his own way. You may already know deep inside things I haven't heard of or thought of yet. All of us come to faith our own way.

Step into the light. Welcome Home.

Printed in the United States
By Bookmasters